On Meanings of Life

On Meanings of Life

Their Nature and Origin

JEROME ECKSTEIN

State University of New York Press

Quotations in chapter 5 from DUINO ELEGIES by Rainer Maria
Rilke, translated by David Young. Copyright © 1978 by W. W.
Norton & Inc. Used by permission of W. W. Norton & Company,
Inc.

Published by State University of New York Press, Albany

© 2002 State University of New York

For information, address State University of New York Press,
90 State Street, Suite 700, Albany, NY 12207

Production by Marilyn P. Semerad
Marketing by Patrick Durocher

Library of Congress Cataloging-in-Publication Data

Eckstein, Jerome.
    On meanings of life : their nature and origin / Jerome Eckstein.
      p. cm.
    Includes bibliographical references and index.
    ISBN 0-7914-5481-9 (alk. paper) — ISBN 0-7914-5482-7
(pbk. : alk. paper)
      1. Life. 2. Meaning (Philosophy) I. Title.

BD435.E25 2002
128—dc21   2002021023

10 9 8 7 6 5 4 3 2 1

To
Jeffrey Berman, W. Scott Hicks,
Howard Joseph, William Weifenbach, and Zack,
and in memory of
Murray Baumel, Harry I. Wohlberg,
and Max Wohlberg

Contents

Acknowledgments

I am grateful to Professor Glenn Dean, John Fairley, Peter Golden, W. Scott Hicks, Rabbi Louis Jacobs, Rabbi Howard Joseph, Donna M. Main, Mari O'Donnell, Kenneth S. O'Neil M.D., Murray Perahia, Rabbi Emanuel Rackman, Professor Irving Rappaport, Professor Melvin I. Urofsky, and Professor Bonnie Veysey for reading the manuscript in whole or in part and for their valuable comments. I alone am responsible for its flaws.

I am especially grateful to Professors Jeffrey Berman and William Weifenbach for their regular, thorough, and insightful criticism (of the manuscript) and for our deep friendship. Jeffrey's help, in particular, went beyond the call of friendship. The book is also dedicated to two other dear friends, to my grandson, and to the memory of my distinguished uncles.

I am most grateful to my wife, Kathleen, for her steadfast love, and for the love of Esther, Mari, and my grandson, Zachary Schwartz.

I am thankful to Kristin Mahar for her secretarial help and to Marilyn A. Penney for preparing the manuscript according to the publisher's specifications.

Introduction

This book started out as another book. A colleague asked me to write a version of my previous book that his students could understand. I began his project with mixed feelings: I was pleased that he thought the previous book important, but I wanted to do something more creative than a rewrite. The desire soon prevailed, and this book emerged—which I trust can be understood by college students.

Nearly all found this book's title piquant on first hearing of it, but their responses were different. Some had assumed that life had only one meaning, *the* meaning of life, and so the plural term, *meanings*, surprised them. Others had assumed that such meaning, or meanings, had been settled since the origin of our species, fixed by God or the cosmos; and so the possible openness of the terms *nature* and *origin* surprised them. Still others said with surprise, perhaps at my audaciousness, that this theme is philosophy's most important question. Hence, I trust that the following brief account of the book's content will begin to demystify the subject.

1

Chapter 1 observes that a contented life requires a relatively even balance between *interests* and *intraests* (in-trästs´), but intraests are much overlooked in our culture; and, thus, meanings of life also tend to go unexamined because they are embodied in intraested involvements. Intraested involvements are non-instrumental, directed at themselves, whereas interested involvements are instrumental, directed at something other than themselves. Both occur along the continuum between their poles and are characterized by the dominant side; they are never pure. Neither is *inherently* superior in being, knowing, or goodness. Work, play, love, art, and neurosis are examined in terms of interests, intraests, and meanings of life.

Chapter 2 argues that both objectivity and subjectivity are required for recognizing our self-deceptions about life meanings and for finding satisfactory meanings. It criticizes those postmodernists who claim a radical subjectivity for all texts as well as those fundamentalists who claim pure objectivity in their reading of Scripture or the Constitution. The Age of Enlightenment is briefly examined because it was then, mainly through the works of Immanuel Kant, that the words *objective* and *subjective* exchanged meanings with each other and received their present meanings. But objectivity and subjectivity, also, occur only along the continuum between their poles, and they are never pure.

Chapter 3 considers the loss and presence of life meanings as causes of suicide and examines in this regard Emile Durkheim's sociological study of suicide—which, a century later, many social scientists still deem relevant. He found that the dissolution of society's common, stable meanings of life, which follows a disequilibrium in social forces and an "excessive individuation," is a major cause for increased rates of suicide, while the presence of life meanings in the suicide norms of societies where "social integration is too strong" and "individuation is insufficient" is another cause of suicide.

I relate Durkheim's account of these causes to Karl Jaspers's later marking of the Axial Age (800–200 B.C.E.). Jaspers notes that before this era people had an organic relation to society, a mythical view of the cosmos, and they followed society's norms automatically or unquestioningly—including suicide norms and life meanings, I would add. But a mature consciousness of individuality, Jaspers observes, arose first in the Axial Age, and that is when, I argue, the meaning of life first emerged as a problem.

Chapter 4 argues that religions and other doctrines cannot furnish their life meanings with objective certainty. They can, at most, stimulate certitude in their followers, a *feeling* of certainty. This is illustrated by a comparison of Orthodox Judaism's right wing with its modern wing, and it applies to conservative and liberal approaches to religion in general.

Chapter 5, inspired by Plato's myths, Rilke's poetry, and the sonata form, traces the biological origin of life meanings to our experience of lost wholeness at birth. Birth exiles us from a secure, contented, and relatively simple world, where we were wholly integrated with our whole world. We can never return to that primordial wholeness; so we seek instead intraested involvements that provide a comprehensive integration, a vicarial wholeness, and such involvements embody our life meanings.

Yet the fear of individuality still drives many automatically or unquestioningly to the established culture for certitude and vicarial wholeness, and only a few confront the problem of life's meaning deliberately, independently, and courageously. I conclude the chapter by arguing against the idea held by some that we are about to enter a Second Axial Age in which our consciousness will be global.

The Epilogue reveals some of my life meanings and discusses them in terms of metaphysical loneliness, metaphysical laughter, and metaphysical dignity.

Chapter 1

Intraestedness and Meanings of Life

Meanings of life are our ultimate values. They are appreciated essentially for themselves alone and not because they subserve another value; indeed, they bestow worth on many other values. Life meanings become embodied in intraested involvements when they pass from disposition to action. What is intraestedness? Let me first give an example. Zachary climbs a mountain mainly because "it is there." The goal of his climb is the climb itself; it is done for its own sake; it is intraested.

He enjoys mountain climbing, and that is his motive for doing it; but intraestedness is concerned only with the activity's goal or direction, and not with its motive—not with the "inner impulse that causes a person to do something." So, I define *intraestedness* as "an act or involvement, conscious or unconscious, that is directed at itself." The word is derived from *intra* and *esse*, "to be involved within."

Interestedness is the complement of intraestedness. For example, Esther climbs a mountain mainly to rescue people. Rescue is the goal or direction of her climb, regardless of motive—whether mercy or greed or whatever. In another example, John uses games in order to inveigle his elementary students into learning; these games are interested. So, I define *interestedness* as "an act or involvement, conscious or unconscious, that is directed at something other than itself." This word is derived from *inter* and *esse*, "to be involved between."

Many languages have a word for *interested*. Its English synonyms are "means," "instrumental," "practical," "pragmatic," "useful," and so forth. But I have not found a positive word in any language with the meanings of *intraested* and its nominal, verbal, adverbial, and substantival forms.

The void is troubling. For we have learned from several disciplines that language shapes, as well as is shaped by, our sense perceptions, thought, values, worldview, and, so, also meanings of life; and different languages shape these differently—sometimes, very differently. Hence, this void in language limits our worldview, our experience of intraestedness, and our possible life meanings.

The matter is even more serious, since English, for instance, disparages the species of *intraestedness*. For example, *Webster's New World Dictionary* defines *wandering* thus: "1. an aimless going about   2. (pl.) travels, esp. when extended and apparently purposeless   3. (pl.) incoherent or disordered thoughts or utterances, as in delirium."

An aura of unfulfillment, failed interests, and mental confusion surrounds this wandering. Unlike the usual sort of going about, the healthy, practical, interested sort—the good sort—*wandering* is defined as "purposeless," "disordered," "delirious," "aimless"; and the latter connotes "showing little or no intelligence." The same applies to *wandering*'s synonyms—*rambling, roving, roaming, meandering,* and *drifting.* This is a sign of our culture's excessive interestedness and, I argue, its diminished life, thought, and life meanings.

Zachary rejects this constricted and biased definition because he wanders intraestedly. He enters the woods without a destination, rambling from path to path, roaming the present, choosing directions spontaneously—moved by hearing a waterfall, smelling wild roses, seeing a deer, feeling pine straw underfoot. He is neither mindless or disordered nor aimless or purposeless. His senses are alive, charmed into impromptu focus; this is what he wanted, wants more of, why he entered the forest. His aim was, is, the involvement itself; he has no goal beyond encountering the woods. He is fulfilled. Intraested wandering deserves a definition that is not pejorative.

But many are still puritans, at least in this respect. Thoreau's 1861 complaint still has relevance:

> If a man walk in the woods for love of them half of each day, he is in danger of being regarded as a loafer; but if he spends his whole day as a speculator, shearing off those woods and making earth bald before her time, he is esteemed an industrious and enterprising citizen. As if a town had no interest in its forests but to cut them down! . . .[1]

This "loafer" is seen as only playing; he does not work as we are obligated to do. He is deemed deficiently interested and having no worthy meaning of life.

Still, a few say that their work is play, and this phrase draws our attention. For most find work and play to be opposites: work is tiresome, requiring sustained effort in order to earn a living or a good hereafter, whereas play is fun, relaxing, usually done for its own sake. Yet many forms of play also require what the dictionary says of work—"sustained effort to overcome obstacles and achieve a result." So that is not why people feel work and play to be opposites.

Does "job satisfaction" inevitably turn work into intraested play or a meaning of life because here the money, power, prestige, and work conditions are good? No; not even a Community of Work ensures this, although it aims at a liberation that is even higher than job satisfaction or enlightened paternalism.

Marcel Barbu and his wife established a Community of Work in the 1940s, which, with its 135 workers, became one of France's seven largest watch-case factories. Not only was its industrial sector altogether democratically determined—the "distinction between employer and employee [was] abolished"—but so was its other main sector, the social sector. The latter had nine chief sections: Spiritual, Intellectual, Artistic, Communitarian Life, Mutual Aid, Family, Health, Sports, and Newspaper. The Community of Work comprised the "wives and the children at home" as well as the workers.[2]

Claire H. Bishop reports that "Barbu was aiming at more than enlightened paternalism. He was after a style of living," a new way of living together. But "very soon," Barbu relates, "we saw the necessity of [acquiring] a common basis, or what we called, from then on, our common ethics." This was not easily accomplished, since the two dozen workers then engaged were comprised of Catholics, Protestants, materialists, humanists, atheists, and communists.[3]

Still, all reexamined their ethics on the basis of what their own experiences and thoughts found necessary, not on what they had been taught by rote or by convention, and "they discovered that their [naturalistic] individual ethics had certain points in common." They adopted these common points as the Community's ethical minimum and formed their own version of the Decalogue—which included, "Thou shalt earn thy bread by the sweat of thy brow."[4]

Yet work was interested even in this exceptional humanistic environment. For "in the Community of Work," a worker wrote, "production is not the aim for living, but the means."[5] Production, work, was not done for its own sake; it was as interested there as in any other factory, although it served a different purpose. It was neither intraested play nor an "aim for living"—i.e., nor a meaning of life.

A. Bartlett Giamatti, scholar of Renaissance literature, president of Yale University, commissioner of baseball, held that, "under the rubric of *leisure*," play as game or sport—"either watched or played—has availed itself fully of whatever prestige or privilege accrues to shared activities that have no purpose except fully to be themselves."[6] Such play is directed to itself. It is intraested, and it has "prestige." Those who say that work is play mean intraested play, play "under the rubric of leisure"; and, for them, work may be also a meaning of life.

For Giamatti knew firsthand that play in professional sport is usually directed otherwise; it is mainly
interested in money. Many "amateurs" also compete
mainly for money, even if not as openly. This is a
recent development, but with ancient roots. The etymology of the word *athlete* goes back to the Greek
athletes, meaning, to contend for a prize. Play is chiefly
an interest for such amateurs, while for others it is
mainly an intraest. Indeed, any act or involvement
can be either interested or intraested; it all depends
on the act's or involvement's direction. Life-meaning
involvements, however, are necessarily intraested, for
they embody our ultimate goals—they are not directed to other goals.

Children's frolic may be the purest sort of
intraested group play; it is in essence carefree, spontaneous, free of firm rules and adult interference. Only
utopians would try to organize frolic. Adult supervision of children's sport, as in Little League baseball,
does not necessarily impair the game's nature as play,
but the adult introduction of extrinsic goals, such as
prizes, does tend to make play interested.

The distinction between act and involvement is
crucial to our judgment of interests and intraests. For
example, baseball comprises many interested acts even
when the game as a whole, as an involvement, is
played intraestedly. Besides acts that are extrinsic
means, such as preparation of bat, ball, and glove,
there are means intrinsic to the game, such as skills,
techniques, and strategies. A pitchout is an interested
act even when the pitcher's involvement in the game
is intraested. Even life-meaning involvements have
interested acts.

The pleasures of the involvement and of the
skillful use of its intrinsic means reinforce each other

when "work is play." The pleasure is much deeper, indeed; it is joy and passion when such work is a life meaning. One who is painting as a life meaning becomes transported: time evanesces, eternity emerges, presentness prevails, and concern for fame or wealth is absent.

Thus, a reviewer notes that Stephen Pace "paints gardens, windjammers and clamdiggers like a choreographer who, in Pam Pace's words, 'stabs, whirls and jabs in very fluid, intuitive motions, followed by calm reflection.'" Pace himself acknowledges that "his lively, technical spontaneity is preceded by long periods of preparation"—of concern with means and imagination, I should think.[7] Spontaneity and mastery merge in such painting; this is a masterful spontaneity.

Interested involvements, correspondingly, comprise many intraested acts. Consider the heavily interested involvement of escape from a burning house. A door appears through the smoke—a sign of possible passage. Simultaneously, though, one notices the door's yellow rectangularity and hears irrelevant street voices. These are intraested perceptions; they are not instrumental to flight. They are intraested acts of an interested involvement.

Indeed, based on Justus Buchler's metaphysics, I have argued that all interested acts as well as involvements have intraested elements, and all intraested acts as well as involvements have interested elements.[8] Note that the door in the above example not only indicates possible escape, but, as Buchler says, "it also is what it is, that sign and no other, making possible the adaptive inference of escape by impressing its qualitative integrity upon attention."[9] The door has the possibility of being an interested sign because it is first accepted intraestedly, qua spectacle, for its qualitative integrity, as that sign and no other. And such is true of every interested act.

But we are also always in part interested. Since "the greater part of [our] life is passed under the relentless pressure to conquer," Buchler says, we "can never escape the general *problem* of stabilization, whether temperamental or environmental."[10] The means for such stabilization function continuously; we have a perpetual interest in stabilization. Hence, acts and involvements are never purely interested or purely intraested; they occur only along a continuum between the poles of interestedness and intraestedness, and they are characterized by the dominant mode.

Furthermore, neither category is inherently superior in terms of ethics. Yet the few philosophers who have approximated these categories—virtually neglected in psychology and other behavioral sciences—have all deemed their versions of intraestedness as ethically superior to interestedness.[11] But that is a mistake.

For example, the Nazis gave work permits to able-bodied Jews, keeping them useful by false hope and thus separated them from the "useless" Jews who were murdered at once. Sometimes the Nazis issued two such permits to Jewish men: one was for themselves only, untransferable, and the other was to be given at their choice either to their able-bodied mother, father, wife, or one child. The Nazis would not make this choice, though that would have produced a better labor force. Jewish men had to decide who among their loved ones was to live and who were to die. Emil L. Fackenheim calls this "a celebration of torture . . . *for torture's* sake"[12]—or, intraested torture. Such "celebration" even embodied a life meaning for some Nazis.

Moreover, interests no less than intraests manifest humanity's unique virtues. Which other earthly species has approximated the benefits of such interests as our law, commerce, science, or technology? An interested grasp of relativity theory dignifies life as much as an intraested appreciation of its elegance. Even the Creator is said to be interested, since life, humanity, and the cosmos are alleged to serve a divine purpose.

So, neither intraestedness nor interestedness is inherently superior in ethics. We must judge the ethics—or aesthetics—of intraests and interests by external standards of value; and this applies also to life meanings. Yet we easily understand the origin of interested involvements—they are the means of survival. But how can we explain the origin of intraested involvements, such as art and the love of beauty?

Jared Diamond considers human history to have "taken off" in a "Great Leap Forward" only some 50,000 years ago because the Neanderthals and their contemporaries were still "less than fully human." He observes that "the earliest definite signs of that leap come from East African sites with standardized stone tools and the first preserved jewelry [ostrich-shell beads]."[13]

The history of fully humans thus begins with advanced interests, standardized multipiece tools for survival, and with intraests, jewelry for adornment or the love of beauty. Such intraested art evolved into the magnificent life-sized paintings of bulls and horses that were created in the Lascaux Cave of southwestern France 25,000 years later. Our explanation is thus simple: intraest in art is as natural to us as interest in survival; intraestedness and interestedness define us equally. Only cultural bias obscures this fact.

I imagine that nature's sporadic eruption sparked a narrow and inchoate sense of individuality in these few early humans when it brought forth their unique gift for painting and jewelry making. The sense, the consciousness of individuality would become widespread, broadened, and developed only in the first millennium B.C.E., for until then a person's relationship to society was organic and mythical. But the early few had a glimmer of individuality and intraested appreciation—and perhaps also of an independent life meaning—even when society adopted their art for religious or political uses and incorporated these into its mythical meaning of life.

Freud sees the origin of art and the love of beauty, however, as interested. Indeed, he views all of civilization interestedly, serving two purposes: "to protect men against nature and to adjust their mutual relations." And yet, he wonders, we count it "as a sign of civilization as well if we see people directing their care to what has no practical value whatever"—for instance, "to reverence beauty . . . and to create it."[14]

Freud's explanation is that since civilization requires us to curb our instincts in order to have satisfactory social relations, we must compensate for the loss of instinctual satisfaction—or else, "serious disorders will ensue." One such compensation occurs when the sexual impulse is "inhibited in its aim," when blocked sexual energy is sublimated (channeled) into the creation or enjoyment of beauty.[15] He thus takes art and the love of beauty to be only interested—as only means to personal and social health.

Freud's explanation, however, has some problems. Why, then, did painting originate with Cro-Magnons and not with the Neanderthals or earlier

Hominidae? They, too, had social regulations to in-
hibit the sexual instinct; but we have neither evidence
of art in their societies, nor signs of "serious [social]
disorders" caused by this lack of compensation.

Furthermore, his explanation is not balanced.
Beauty strikes me as also an original love, not only
one met on the rebound; also a first choice, not only
a compensation; also rooted in nature, not only in
civilization. Indeed, animals may also have an
intraested sense of beauty.[16] Even Freud doubts the
extent of civilization's inhibitive role in the development of art.[17]

Henri Bergson, however, sees the origin of art
and the love of beauty as intraested. He observes that
"now and then, by a lucky accident, men arise whose
senses or whose consciousness are less adherent to
life," whose perception is less attached to action, to
utility. "They perceive in order to perceive—for nothing, for the pleasure of doing so"; they love color for
itself and form for itself. They are "born *detached*;
and according to whether this detachment is that of
a particular sense, or of consciousness, they are paint-
ers or sculptors, musicians or poets." The artist has
"therefore a much more direct vision of reality," and
"he perceives a greater number of things."[18] This is
a natural detachment, a natural intraest—one innate
in the structure of sense or consciousness; it is not
merely a compensation required by civilization.

But most of us, Bergson notes, have a greater
attachment to life. Our senses and consciousness "iso-
late that part of reality as a whole that interests us,"
and they "show us less the things themselves than
the use we can make of them." They "classify" and
"label" things beforehand; "we scarcely look at the

object, it is enough for us to know to which category it belongs." The individuality of things or beings escapes us.[19] Most of us are nearly always interested.

Much in Bergson's account of beauty's origin wins my assent, but his account, too, is neither balanced nor unbiased. Yes, we must be "detached" from "practical reality" in order to perceive beauty; but interest in the means to beauty is essential for the artist, and recognizing the means affords the cognoscenti a greater appreciation of beauty. Bergson's explanation is not sufficiently balanced.

Neither is it unbiased. Yes, detachment reveals a special aspect of reality; but it neither is an inherently superior way of knowing, nor does it disclose a superior reality. Bergson's bias, which is shared by the other versions of our categories, sees intraests as giving "a much more direct vision of reality," as penetrating to the "inner life of things," to the "actual things themselves," whereas interests merely read the "labels" affixed to the actual things.

I emphasize, therefore, that neither interestedness nor intraestedness is inherently superior in ethics, or in knowing, or in being. Moreover, no life-meaning involvement is inherently superior in these respects.

The idea that one reality is "more" real than another reality is meaningless to me. What does "real" mean if there are degrees to reality? Anything encountered is for me real, and equally real with anything else encountered. Fiction is as real as history, dreams are as real as bones, and life meanings are as real as buildings; they just belong to different orders of reality. There is what Justus Buchler calls "ontological parity," not "ontological priority."

Yet it is meaningful to say that one part or order of reality is in some situations more powerful or more valuable or more important than another part or order of reality. A novel is sometimes more powerful and more valuable and more important than an act of Congress, whereas the converse is true in other situations; but they are equally real in either case. And it makes sense, too, that different ways of knowing are respectively better suited for different orders of reality; but none of these ways is inherently superior.

Bergson's "idealistic" ontological bias, favoring the "inner life of things" over their external "labels," is in our culture a minority viewpoint. The "realistic" ontological bias, favoring the external, the materialistic, the spatial, is in our culture the majority's viewpoint. These biases are directly related to respectively different meanings of life.

Our dominant materialistic bias is reflected in the dictionary's following definition: "imaginary applies to that which exists in the imagination only and is, therefore, unreal." It "exists," but it is "unreal"! It is not material, and it is "therefore" unreal! Would you who feel love say that it is unreal? Would you who believe in an immaterial deity say that God is immaterial in the dictionary's secondary sense—"unimportant, not pertinent"? Do you think that the primary definition of *immaterial* as "incorporeal" did not lead to the word's secondary definition as "unimportant"? No; and because life meanings are merely "immaterial, inner" issues, few nowadays reflect on them.

Indeed, apart from play or entertainment, the populace is rarely involved with intraests, even though intraestedness is an innate need. This explains the exorbitant monies paid to entertainers. Talk of morals, politics, or religion, however, is chiefly predilection, promotion of interests. Partiality prevails, objectivity is attenuated, and truth is neglected.

Some never fault partiality because they argue that objectivity is impossible. Yet my students and I noticed that Madonna was not present in our class yesterday to deliver a lecture on kabbalah, and no postmodernist can persuade us to doubt her absence. It was objectively so, even though our images and feelings about her likely differed. Otherwise, she could sue the college for a fee.

Our experience of objectivity always has a subjective side since it is our experience; it always comprises some feelings, values, or attitudes. And subjectivity always has an objective side, since its context is the person's world; it always alludes to some fact or occurrence. Dreams concern not only our psyches, but also some happenings of the day and of years past. Life meanings, too, have an objective side that reflects the history that formed them. We are never purely subjective or objective; as with interests and intraests, subjectivity and objectivity occur only along the continuum between their respective poles, and they are named after the dominant side.

I mean by *objectivity* the attempt to encounter anything as it is, and not as wished or imagined. I mean it in accordance with its Latin etymology, as *something thrown in our way*, resisting us, but not as apart from perspective, context, or the premises of language and thought.

Objectivity is the most effective approach for interests, whether mining, medicine, or politics. In psychotherapy, too, one examines the wish that was, not what one wishes it to have been. Objectivity is from a different perspective or context essential also to intraests, whether in playing the piano or in regarding one's son as an end in himself. Beauty is not in the ignorant eye or ear. A life meaning is the hardest intraest to change, since its range is the deepest and most comprehensive; but an overpowering event, such as the Holocaust, may cause one to reexamine a life meaning objectively and replace it.

Meanings of life, as long as they prevail, are our ultimate, final values; they validate other values, and the others cannot validate them. We rest in the wholeness of these meanings, which requires them to be consummated, embodied, fulfilled in the completeness of intraested involvements; interested involvements, though, are directed to values beyond their involvements, and those values may require validation and fulfillment by other values and involvements, and so on. Hence, the values of interests, too, can obtain *ultimate, final* fulfillment only in intraested involvements.

One thus finds ultimate consummation only in intraestedness. The Torah's concept of the Sabbath reflects this principle (Exodus 20:8–11). The six days of interested work, of "subduing the earth," are fulfilled in a Sabbath of holy, intraested rest. The ancient rabbis were puzzled by the opposition between "and He rested on the seventh day" (Exodus 20:11) and "God finished his work on the seventh day" (Genesis 2:2), for the latter implies that not all had been created in six days. A rabbi answered: "What was created on the seventh day? Tranquility, serenity, peace and repose" (Genesis Rabbah 10:9).

Matter was released from the law of inertia on metamorphosing into life and bound to an opposite law. Newton recognized inertia as a property of matter whereby matter remains at rest or in uniform motion in the same straight line unless acted upon by some external force. But life is a property of matter whereby generation and cessation occur even if not acted upon by an external force. And in human life, generation and cessation seek consummation in intraests and, especially, in meanings of life.

The price of life is death: a loss of the infinitesimal possibility of inorganic matter's endless and unchanging existence, of its never being acted on by an external force. Living matter becomes worn out from the continual generation and cessation, and hence death is natural—it does not necessarily result from accident or disease or, in the case of humans, from sin. The price of human life is, besides death, the knowledge of approaching death, the likelihood of unhappiness, and the possibility of finding life meaningless.

Knowledge of death's inevitability would make life meaningless for many were it not for their belief in immortality. Yet Miguel de Unamuno, a believer, admits that "within its limits" reason proves the impossibility of "the individual consciousness . . . persist[ing] after the death of the physical organism upon which it depends." What we actually desire of immortality "is not merely spiritual felicity . . . but bodily happiness," yet that cannot be. And "even if by a mighty effort of faith" we overcome this argument of reason, the idea of the soul's endless life "involves us in [other] contradictions and absurdities."[20]

Still, despite the absurdities, "we must needs believe in that other life that we may live this life, and endure it, and give it meaning and finality." Unamuno sees the struggle between reason and faith as God-given, as "two enemies, neither of which can maintain itself without the other." He concludes his book with a prayer on our behalf: "And may God deny you peace, but give you glory!"[21] Only belief in an afterlife brings meaning to this life for Unamuno, but he emphasizes that it ought to be an uneasy belief because reason's objectivity persistently and rightly throws obstacles in the way of that belief and life meaning.

But others deny objectivity a proper role in the determination of faith's life meaning; they argue that the exercise of one's reason here is a self-willed, selfish resistance to God. Their argument rests on several faults, however, one of which is a confusion between self-interest and selfishness. I argue, though, that deliberation over meanings of life is much needed and that it is self-interested but not selfish.

Interestedness and intraestedness prevail strictly when something other than the agent is the subject of the act's or involvement's goal. On climbing a mountain to rescue a child, the child is the subject of the interested climb's goal; and on climbing a mountain intraestedly, the mountain is the subject of the climb's goal.

But self-interestedness and self-intraestedness prevail when the agent is the subject of the act's or involvement's goal. I am self-interested on freely associating ideas and feelings in psychotherapy or in writing a novel, and I am self-intraested on drifting along my unfettered mind, marvelling at its bizarre turns, blind to consequences, whether Freudian or Joycean.

Ordinary usage and the dictionary banefully confound self-interest with selfishness. Yet both agree that selfishness is being "*too much* concerned with one's own interests and having *little* or *no* concern for others." Why do they then not see that working for one's living or caring for one's health is normally self-interested but not selfish?

My definition of *self-interestedness*, however, avoids identification with *selfishness*, since it allows for non-selfishness and unselfishness as well as selfishness; it requires only that the agent be the subject of an act or involvement that is directed to something other than the act or involvement. Hence, selfishness is necessarily self-interested, but self-interestedness is not necessarily selfish.

Ordinary usage and the dictionary also confound self-love with selfishness because they view self-love in terms of their confused idea of self-interest. The confusion results from a tendency to assign valuational and descriptive meanings to the same word—in this case, to self-interest. We should not be surprised, therefore, that some have denigrated self-love.

For instance, Paul Brownback, Evangelical theologian, asks in his book *The Danger of Self-Love:* "Even if we agree that man has worth because he is in God's image, the question remains, does that give him the right to feel *good* about himself?" Citing Paul (1 Corinthians 1:31) and mistranslating Jeremiah (9:22–23) for support, he answers in the negative: "Not only is the Bible silent when it comes to any encouragement to 'feel good' about ourselves, but one of its major themes is that we should not boast in self but in the Lord."[22]

Now, an objective gulf exists between boasting in self and feeling good about self, but Brownback overlooks it. Boasting is by definition "showing too much pride and satisfaction—bragging"; it is often neither honest nor salutary, whether it concerns oneself or others. Brownback lacks objectivity here, and this makes his idea of self-love feeble and simplistic; since a love that includes self-love has proved to be a healthy meaning of life.

For instance, the Golden Rule as found in the Torah and the Gospels approves of self-love. The Torah (Leviticus 19:18) says, "love thy neighbor *as* thyself"; while the Gospel (Matthew 7:12) says, "always treat others as you would like them to treat you—that is the Law (Torah) and the Prophets." But the Gospels (Mark 12:28–34, Luke 10:25–28, Matthew 22:34–40) also preach the Golden Rule by quoting Leviticus's version. Both versions imply a healthy and genuine self-love, one that is not selfish. Indeed, the Golden Rule itself entails an opposition between self-love and selfishness, for "love of neighbor" rules out selfishness.

The Golden Rule is more than a precept; it is a meaning of life. Thus, the Talmud (Shabbath 31a) relates that a heathen said to Hillel (of the generation before Jesus): "You may convert me, but on condition that you teach me the whole Torah while I stand on one foot." The sage replied, putting the Golden Rule in a negative form: "What is hateful to you, do not to your neighbor: that is the whole Torah, while the rest is its commentary; go and learn it."[23] And Jesus promises "eternal life" (Luke 10:25–28) and entry to "the kingdom of God" (Mark 12:28–34) to all who obey the Golden Rule and the command to love God with all one's might (Deut. 6:5).

The Golden Rule is also a secular life meaning, discovered in natural experience. For example, Erich Fromm finds that love is a life meaning for the emotionally healthy person; that "the love for [one's] own self is inseparably connected with the love for any other self"; and that "*selfishness and self-love . . . are actually opposites.*" The selfish person merely "makes an unsuccessful attempt to cover up and compensate for his failure to care for his real self."[24] Inadequate objectivity thus deceives some who believe that self-love is their life meaning.

Love also is interested when it is directed to the future, when one hopes for a return or some other consequence; such love may be unrequited. And love is intraested when it is directed to the present, when one simply delights in the beloved's presence without concern for a return or consequence; such love may be unreciprocated but not unrequited.

William Wordsworth writes of "Being crazed in brain / by unrequited love." The anxiety and frustration that are often parts of love arise from its concern with the future, and they are absent when love is intraested. Alas, psychologists have generally overlooked intraestedness; consequently, the nature of a complete love, in which intraests and interests are more evenly balanced, is as yet inadequately appreciated.

For instance, Leon Salzman's authoritative book on the obsessive personality hardly notices the role of intraestedness in its view of a "mature person's" experience of time—and thus, by inference, in the experience of love. The obsessive is directed to the future because of an exorbitant need to control, to be interested. Hence, the obsessive's awareness of the present tends to be "superficial and cursory," whereas recall tends to be "inadequate, sketchy"—because "the past is a collection of 'presents.' " "Unlike the mature person," the obsessive cannot use an understanding of the past to lead the present into a future.[25] There is no mention of the mature person's intraested present.

For the hysteric, however, "only the present moment has any reality." Salzman notes that this person has a great distrust of the future, and is only "interested in the *effect* his performance is achieving at this moment." The hysteric has only a small capacity to postpone gratification, and hence "must grab all he can right now."[26] This focus on the present is limited to the hysteric's interest.

For the depressed person, however, "time exists only as it transpired in the past." Salzman observes that the depressed person perceives the present as being without value and the future as being without possibility; "time has stopped, . . . and the passage of time is a burden that he cannot surmount."[27] This focus on the past is not intraested.

All of these neurotics are exorbitantly interested. One can infer from this that the emotionally healthy person manifests a more even balance of interestedness and intraestedness. But Salzman intimates only once that the "mature person" enjoys an intraested present: he says critically of the obsessive that "the present does not seem to exist for itself."[28] Much more needs to be observed objectively about the psychological necessity of intraestedness for a healthy life and a healthy meaning of life.

Let us summarize this chapter's observations on the nature of life meanings: (1) They are our ultimate values, and they are embodied in intraested involvements. Like all intraested involvements, they have interested acts. (2) They influence more choices in more of our being's dimensions than any other value; they are our widest ranging values. (3) Two profound possibilities follow: if life-meaning involvements are fulfilled, then their satisfaction is deeper and wider than that of any other involvement; and if they are regularly blocked, then life feels worthless, even to the point of committing suicide. (4) Life-meaning involvements, like all other intraested involvements, are inherently neither superior nor inferior to interested or other intraested involvements in knowledge or being or value. (5) Finally, objectivity has an important role in the determination and abandonment of life meanings.

Still, objective argument cannot logically persuade one who disvalues health to abandon an unhealthy life meaning. And some would argue that objective argument cannot logically persuade even one who values health to abandon an unhealthy life meaning because they believe that objectivity is impossible. I have already indicated my opposition to this view, but I examine it at greater length in chapter 2.

Chapter 2

Excursus to Objectivity and Postmodernism

A friend raises the following objection to chapter 1. He agrees with the postmodernist argument against objectivity, and thus thinks that my confidence in Madonna's absence from my class is too strong. My friend's objection likely stems from a sensitive soul's tendency to idealize subjectivism in reaction to a crass and narrow objectivism. His sensitivity appeals to me, but not his idealization.

That issue is this chapter's main subject, for I wish to show that both a moderate objectivism and a temperate subjectivism are important in the formation and rejection of life meanings. The nature of the opposition between the postmodernists and their critics behooves me to shed a personal light on my position. I have long learned to sense in philosophy both the subjective and the objective, the emotional

27

and the rational, and so I begin with the following brief account of my journey.

Vague, censored, ambiguous, conflicting parental communication of feeling made it difficult for me in childhood to identify emotions directly, mine and others'. What did the complex of words, silences, and gestures mean? This moved me to roundabout routes of identification, one of which began in the gateway of ideas and beauty.

This route led to the quiet Cordovan neighborhood of Averroës's and Maimonides's boyhood, respectively the greatest medieval rationalists of Islam and Judaism—streets where sunlight falls softly on small white houses with flowers on every balcony, senses and soul suffused with clarity and peace; it brought me to Toledo, still medieval, to El Greco's and Samuel Halevi's house, also harmonious, though darker, more angular, from which celestial longing erupts like a geyser; it took me to Granada's Alhambra, sublime structure of gardens and rooms lined with Moorish geometric designs on varicolored ceramic tiles, many faded, bordered by a whispering canal, architecture that still engenders bliss, still fuses reason with emotion.

These ideal houses delighted me—especially their music rooms, playgrounds, and libraries of Talmud and philosophy. Only later would I come upon the inevitable hidden underground passageway behind the bookcase and find that the texts always had an emotional as well as a rational dimension. *Aleph* would be revealed in *bet*.

Meanwhile, however, clarity, literality, and consistence dominated every intellectual concern, but the understanding that much of their force came from a need for straightforwardness in emotional communication escaped me. Thus, when my father and uncle regaled each other with their midrashic creations on Scripture, I, though yet religious and cognizant of Midrash's ancient and holy tradition, was silently annoyed; for the midrashic method is nonliteral— allusive, allegoric, and homiletic.

My father and uncle were gifted in Midrash— indeed, my uncle, Rabbi Harry I. Wohlberg, taught Midrash at Yeshiva University—and they smiled in delight at each other's flights of fancy. I appreciated their inventiveness, but how could they believe that God's intentions were revealed through such play and games? Divine communication had to be logical for me—either plain scriptural meaning, or halakhic (legalistic) or theological articulation.

I did not know what my father and uncle presumably knew, that Maimonides (1135–1204) had viewed the Midrashim as "poetical conceits" only and "not meant to bring out the meaning of the text in question." Nor did I know what my father and uncle definitely knew, that Abraham ibn Ezra (d. 1167) had viewed the homiletical Midrashim only figuratively, for they "can hardly be taken literally."[1]

When the Holocaust killed my religious faith, philosophy became my path toward a meaning of life. But its prevailing schools did not attract me, even though they were the chief routes to the philosophical career that I sought. Analytic philosophy and logical positivism had abandoned philosophy's traditional search for wise meanings of life, so I had to find my own way.

Reading psychology and undergoing psychotherapy led me to the secret underground passageway behind the books where hidden meanings stir. Philosophic acts of ferreting presuppositions, sensing needed qualifications, recognizing inconsistencies, and perceiving odd choices of words now illuminated the biases or conflicts at work in the author's underground. Both levels of the text had to be examined.

Later, Henri Bergson and Benjamin Lee Whorf led me to another underground channel of meaning—the linguistic. Both saw language as providing forms that shape our sense perceptions and thoughts, but Whorf saw also that different languages with their distinct forms shape our world differently. Language is thus not merely passive in describing facts; it contributes to the formation and constitution of facts. Yet this "does not mean that it *produces* the fact," Friedrich Waismann emphasized in 1945.[2]

Lectures on Plato's *Republic* by a great teacher and scholar, John H. Randall, Jr., led me to yet another underground channel of meaning in philosophy—the dramatic. He saw in some Platonic dialogues an essential unity of drama and philosophy, where the two modify each other and form a new genre—the theater of ideas. Yet Plato's magnificent genre had gone unrecognized for more than two millennia.

Granted, his drama and philosophy were supremely esteemed, but separately. Alfred N. Whitehead so valued Plato's philosophy that he considered the entire European philosophical tradition as "consist[ing] of a series of footnotes to Plato."[3] Whereas R. Hackforth lauded Plato's *Phaedo* as "a work of supreme art, perhaps the greatest achievement in Greek prose literature," and R. S. Bluck extolled that dialogue as "a masterpiece of dramatic literature."

Yet none of them saw the dialogue's drama and philosophy as integrated. Hackforth assumed that the dialogue's "framework," the events as distinct from the philosophic conversation, is "factual," and so he

missed the framework's dramatic–philosophic significance.[4] Whereas Bluck had to protect his profession's
self-assigned supremacy by giving voice to its universal conviction: Plato had "undoubtedly intended the
Phaedo to be first and foremost a work of philosophy"; and "by approaching his works primarily as
philosophy we are likely to discover much more of
the mind and personality of the author, and of his
achievement against the background of his age." The
drama is mere adornment.[5]

None had seen that Plato's unique method is to
make drama and philosophy interdependent throughout the dialogue. But then Randall showed that, by
giving the drama its due, the *Republic* becomes an
argument against utopianism, and not, as is the universal view, an argument for utopianism.[6] The logic
of Randall's demonstration led me to write two books
on the Platonic method, but it was Plato's demonstration of perfectionism's self-destructiveness that
moved me to do so. Reason and emotion, objectivity
and subjectivity, united in me as they did in the dialogue, and a meaning of life was changed.

So, radical postmodernists ought not to dismiss
me as some Neanderthal objectivist of the modern
period who is insensitive to the poetry of words, the
ambiguity of acts, and the subjective dimension of all
behavior. But I know that Madonna was not in our
classroom that day; sanity demands this, and I intend
to approach the nature of life meanings with a sane,
balanced objectivity.

Some postmodernists deny the value of sanity,
however, or at least this concept of sanity, and reason
cannot disprove their claim—for they deny the possibility of objectivity. Yet most of them are not so
immune to objectivity as to flout it in practice, despite

their investment in theory. They avoid oncoming traffic and do not deconstruct the "text" of traffic signals, and they apparently communicate with each other in some sort of writing. Still, a heavy subjectivism is widespread in various parts of culture, some of which I now examine.

The main concern of Mordecai M. Kaplan, founder of Jewish Reconstructionism, was to bring Judaism into accord with modern knowledge, and so he reprehended Midrash as still practiced in 1937 for being anachronistic. He did not blame premodern rabbis for "ascribing meanings to the traditional content of a religion or social heritage which could neither have been contemplated nor implied by the authors of that content"—a type of Midrash or interpretation he called *transvaluation*, in a sense different from Nietzsche's. For they lacked our methods of historical research, and thus could not recognize anachronisms. Moreover, their Midrash enabled the Jewish religion to adapt and grow.

But modern Midrash's approach to the text should be a *revaluation*: a balance of objectivity and subjectivity in "disengaging from the traditional content those elements [and implications] . . . which answer permanent postulates of human nature, and . . . integrating them into our own ideology." The implications need not be such that the premoderns would have been able to articulate, but they should be psychologically akin to what the premoderns did articulate.[7]

Yet much rabbinic Midrash is still transvaluational, sixty years after Kaplan's criticism. It prevailed until recently even in Reform Judaism, despite that movement's continuous goal of accommodating Judaism to reason and modernity. Gary Bretton-

Granatoor, a leading Reform rabbi, observes: "Now we realize we're in the business of religious action, not social action," but "in the '80s we supported any major liberal political proposition and then would search through the Bible for a tag line we could glue onto it to make it look like a Jewish cause."[8]

Such rabbis are postmodern transvaluators because they knowingly disregard the Author's intention. Their use of a sermonic "tag line" is deceitful to the congregation; it camouflages rabbinic subjectivity as objectivity. Their duplicity disturbs me, but then, honest, perceptive, and humanistic Midrash is not easy to achieve.

Transvaluation is at home in the U.S. Supreme Court as well as in the synagogue and church. Both strict constructionists and liberal constructionists ("judicial activists") have at times transvaluated the U.S. Constitution: the latter by reading it loosely, and the former by adhering strictly to its original application, while both disregard or contravene in such cases the Constitution's original meaning. Both camouflage judicial subjectivity as objectivity.

All meaning is derived from context, and the Constitution's original meaning is derived from the Founding Fathers' social, historical, economic, religious, and legal contexts. The Constitution's original application pertained to its original meaning, but later contexts sometimes required different applications in order to realize the original meaning, and future contexts will most likely require the same. This is also true for meanings of life.

Justice David H. Souter approaches the Constitution thus, and so he is neither a strict nor liberal constructionist. He says: "On constitutional matters, I am of the interpretivist school. We're not looking for the original application, we're looking for [original] meaning here. That's a very different thing."[9] Souter strives to revaluate the Constitution and not to transvaluate it. He shies from the deep subjectivity of some liberal constructions and from the shallow objectivity of some strict constructions. Yet just as the Constitution's original meanings sometimes require amendment, so do life meanings.

The three approaches to the Constitution have parallels in three approaches to the Bible, and the Age of Enlightenment (eighteenth century) is central to our historical understanding of these approaches; for it was then that the words *subjective* and *objective* received their present meanings by exchanging meanings with each other, which indicated an essential difference between modernity and premodernity.

The *Oxford English Dictionary* (OED) notes under the word *objective* that, when "opposed to *subjective* in the older [premodern] sense," it had signified what "exist[s] as an object of consciousness as distinct from [what has] any real existence." It was the word *subjective* which in the older sense had signified what is "presented to the mind as it is, or may be, in itself or its own nature." The OED cites instances from 1325 to 1744.

The OED next notes that when "opposed to *subjective* in the modern sense," the word *objective* signifies "the object of perception or thought, as distinct from the perceiving or thinking subject; a 'thing' external to the mind; real." A few transitional instances of this meaning are found in the later seventeenth and early eighteenth centuries, "but its current use appears to be derived from Kant, and to appear in Eng. subsequently to 1790, and chiefly after 1817."

B. A. G. Fuller observes that "no system in the history of philosophy has had so immediately widespread and profound an effect" as that of Immanuel Kant (1724–1804)—indeed, "the next hundred years were almost completely dominated by it." Bertrand Russell and John H. Randall, Jr., agree with Fuller,[10] so it is prima facie plausible that the exchange of meanings derives from Kant. But let us look deeper.

Kant argued that the world is unknowable as it is in itself, that we perceive and understand it only through the medium of our mind's innate forms and categories. We see a bird in flight only when the mind's innate forms of space and time shape the matter of sensation supplied by nature, but we cannot perceive the "bird" or "flight" as they are in themselves. We understand the relation between the bird's soaring and the air currents only when the mind's innate category of causality arranges our perceptions. We do not know the world passively; our mind is the agent of knowledge. And since we all share the same forms and categories, they can provide what he called *objective* knowledge.

Kant had to reject the prevailing meaning of *subjective* as that which is "presented to the mind as it is in itself." First, knowledge is not "presented" to a passive mind, and, second, that which is in itself, what he called *noumena*, is unknowable. He used the word *phenomena* to denote the world that we know through our forms and categories.

Why did Kant not keep the word *subjective* as a sign of truth or reason and replace its old meaning with his phenomenal meaning? Perhaps he felt that only a striking change of the term that signifies truth would bring his truth to the public's attention. In any case, he gave the sign of truth and reason to the word *objective*, to that which has intersubjective validity, and he relegated the word *subjective* to be a sign of the self's private realm.

Kant founded morality, too, on a priori laws derived from reason, but also on an internal sense of moral obligation. He believed that the world beyond science's reach is essentially a universal moral order; that the will is autonomous, free to follow reason's moral laws in defiance of psychological causes; and that reason should also inspire the state toward the equality of citizens. And so, he welcomed the French Revolution.

The defining ideals of the Enlightenment, of modernity, coalesced in Kant's philosophy—the attack on tradition and authority, and the embracement of reason, universality, objectivity, equality, humanism, autonomy, and the agency of mind. Even faith has tended to be severed from subjective experience "since the beginning of the modern age," thus making mystical union suspect; for it was then, Louis Dupré notes, that "theology had begun to separate the universal element of experience implicit in the original idea of grace from the privileged consciousness of union attained by few."[11]

Hence, a sociologist concludes, "Kant is acknowledged to have inaugurated the modern age."[12] Yes, but he did not start it. The physical sciences were already modern, and, as Randall adds in *The Making of the Modern Mind*: "It is in the building up of a science of man, perhaps even more in the very vision of the possibilities and necessity of such a science, that the eighteenth century can rest its soundest claim to important achievement."[13]

Enlightenment ideals were already life meanings for many before Kant wrote. Many American colonists gave their life for these meanings, and the author of the Declaration of Independence could expect that Europe would understand and sympathize with its proclamation: "We hold these truths to be self-evident, that all men are created equal, that they are endowed by their Creator with certain unalienable Rights, that among these are Life, Liberty and the pursuit of Happiness."

Most intellectuals took the rapid and far-flung development of science and technology since the mid-nineteenth century as proof that objectivity is reason's standard—that it is the main gate to reality and the best road to the commonweal. But the uses of science and technology for the unprecedented, vast destruction of human life in World War I and II and the Holocaust in the twentieth century, and their possible use for a global nuclear destruction, disillusioned many with modernity, reason, objectivity, and humanism and brought on postmodernity.

But what exactly is postmodernism? Is it a movement opposed to modernism, or is it a development of modernism?

The first question is easily answered: *postmodernism* is not a precise term. The practitioners of deconstruction, one of postmodernism's chief manifestations, explicitly disdain the precision of a definition; they refuse to categorize their practice with any definite noun, such as *theory* or *method* or *philosophic project*. Jacques Derrida, deconstructionism's founder, says: "All sentences of the type 'deconstruction is X' . . . a priori miss the point."[14] Deconstructionists thus disdain objectivity, and we are not surprised that *deconstruction* has many different and even contradictory meanings.[15]

Indeterminacy is true of postmodernism in general. For example, Brian S. Turner notes that "although

postmodernism has often been associated with
neoconservatism, . . . an important alliance [exists] between progressive politics (in gender issues, multi-
cultural alternatives to racism, in ecology movements
and cultural criticism) and postmodernism."[16]

Another indeterminacy revolves about the relation between sociology and postmodernism: whether
to strive for a sociology of postmodernism, or for a
postmodern sociology. Advocates of the former, Turner
notes, place postmodern culture "in a context of disorganized capitalism, of consumer society and cultural
mass production," and they approach this "crisis"
through traditional assumptions and analyses, while
advocates of the latter "deconstruct [destroy] such
foundational assumptions, and . . . regard 'the social'
as problematic."[17]

Because the postmodern sociologists represent
modernity by horrible events and wicked institutions,
they see their radical antimodernism as progressive
and their opponents' position as reactionary. But the
sociologists of postmodernism see modernity as a
worthy humanistic project to be completed by
postmodernism, so they consider their approach to
be progressive and their opponents' approach to be
reactionary.[18] This answers my second question, and
it coheres with the answer to my first question.

Sociologists of postmodernism use objective,
social science methods. Thus, Lieteke van Vucht
Tijssen observes that "for the social sciences postmodernism seems to be nothing less or more than a
fashionable disguise for good old theories like social
constructivism, symbolic interactionism and critical
cultural analysis."[19] Even those sociologists of
postmodernism who infect their methods with preju-
dice claim objectivity.

But postmodern sociologists cannot credibly claim objectivity, nor do they wish to do so. *Objectivity* is a dirty word for them. Their goal is not social science; it is political counteraction against the ideals and practices of modernity. Hence, Barry Smart argues, *postmodern sociology* is "a contradiction in terms," and its followers should "abandon its generalizing social science ambitions."[20]

The same debate occurs in postmodern feminist studies. For example, Judith Plaskow takes the radical position: "Feminist theology in particular . . . make[s] it amply clear that *all* thinkers have special interests and that claims to objectivity serve *only* to disguise the interests of scholars who are generally involved in serving the status quo"; for "the notion of the detached, disinterested scholar [is] a dangerous myth."[21] I suppose that she sees her own position, also, as having no objective truth, as incapable of sustaining her generalizations.

Hava Tirosh-Rothschild, however, takes a moderate position. She notes that although, "initially, some feminist thinkers embraced radical subjectivism," later, "feminists came to realize that relativism is not only self-contradictory, but also politically counterproductive." For "if there is no objective social reality, how can feminists claim that women's oppression is real?"[22] I favor her moderateness, but many "feminists . . . [still] embrace radical subjectivism." Also, I wish that she had not identified relativism with subjectivism.

Eugene B. Borowitz, Reform theologian, claims to have written "the first full-scale postmodern theory of Judaism," but one that is "non-Derridean." Still, he, too, believes that objectivity is impossible: "With 'objectivity' unattainable," he says, "religious . . . particularity now has a proper role in thinking."[23] The quotation marks surrounding *objectivity* emphasize his disbelief in its possibility. Yet he does not reject science. He does slight science, however. He says that science is now "increasingly viewed" as only one way of accounting for the natural order and that we may find better ways of doing that. But he is not yet ready to scrap science. It is still "too efficacious . . . for us to spurn it for the . . . superstitions of prior ages or for the unverifiable speculations of contemporary antiscientific visionaries."[24] Yet modernists would argue that science is "efficacious" because it is objective, and that the antiscientific speculations are ineffective because they are "unverifiable," subjective. So why does Borowitz speak of objectivity as futile?

Borowitz does so because he is a modernist trying, unsuccessfully, to be a postmodernist. He takes objectivity in a modernistic sense of a correspondence to reality, but unlike most modernists, he takes it to be a pure, perfect, or absolute representation of reality; and so he concludes, in agreement with the postmodernists, that objectivity is unattainable.

But conceiving of objectivity as pure or absolute is a mistake. Objectivity and subjectivity are ever copresent, always a matter of degree or balance. Experience is formed only by the union of perspective and scene, attitude and horizon, subjectivity and objectivity. The idea of encountering the world free of perspective or context or subjectivity is as meaningless as the idea of a round square. So why take objectivity in a way that it cannot be actualized?[25]

Reform or Liberal Judaism arose in the Enlightenment, and for a century and a half assumed the age's dogmas of pure reason, absolute objectivity, and human perfectibility—until the Holocaust caused some liberals to abjure them. Alas, they should have kept their trust in reason, objectivity, perhaps even in humanity, and relinquished their faith in purity, absoluteness, and perfectibility. But they needed this faith to still their relentless yearning for certainty. Borowitz, too, rejects objectivity rather than take it as limited because he also yearns for certainty.

He says as much: "The postmodern search for a substitute *absolute began as* it became clear ['by the social disarray and moral anarchy around us'] that modernity had betrayed our faith." He blames philosophers for abetting morality's debasement "by their . . . identification of *certainty* with scientific method and the rational with the verifiable."[26] But the blame is unwarranted because philosophers have known for more than two centuries that science yields probabilities and not certainties.

Three short quotations illuminate the underground of Borowitz's argument. "With human reason itself also suspect, our civilization has lost its once *rock-solid ground* of value." "The *ground* of secular ethics slowly collapsed." The postmodern religious "sense the reality of a [transcendent] God who *grounds* our values yet . . . calls human beings into an active partnership."[27] He uses the word *ground* dozens of times in this connection, which indicates his yearning for rock-solid certainty. But, alas, our ground, our Earth, is only a floating space station stabilized by attraction.

That stability, however, provides much reliable, objective knowledge. But Derrida denies that any stabilized station exists outside the space of language, and so every structure is collapsible—whether it be an economy, a science, or a news report; for all structures are texts, built on vulnerable premises and supported by shaky pillars of interpretation. Deconstruction's function is to expose, undermine, and destroy all foundations. It cannot reach any stable conclusion because it must not settle on any premise.

Life must seem like fiction to resolute deconstructionists, since no firm facts, values, or truths exist for them—not even truths revealed by fiction or deconstruction. Theoretically, they ought to have no durable meaning of life, but they do—even if it is only an intraest in deconstruction. Ideally, they ought to have no lasting interest, but they do—otherwise, they would soon die by resignation. They cannot continuously play and deconstruct intraestedly, for life requires active interests in survival.

And the deconstructionists have been good at professional survival. Michel Foucault described Derrida's manner of writing as an effort at "obscurantist terrorism," an effort that his followers have emulated. David Lehman explains: "The idea is that the style is so obscure that it's hard to know what the author is trying to say, and this allows the savant to heap contempt on his critics by saying they have failed to understand him." This effort has been very successful in academia against departmental foes and others,[28] despite the fact that many academics are themselves no slouches at obscurantic writing.

Other postmodernists are less radical. They openly and unconditionally accept the value of liberation from some political or intellectual domination toward whose end they deconstruct. But they, too, deny the possibility of objectivity because they still think of it as a pure, direct perception of a solid world that can be expressed in a transparent language. Yet that notion of objectivity has been discredited since Kant.

For example, Ferdinand de Saussure described the linguistic structures that precede all thought and that make representation possible; Claude Lévi-Strauss noted basic social structures that regulate social interaction; Karl Marx showed how economic interests influence spiritual values; Freud illuminated the psyche's dark forces that shape and often distort experience; and the list could go on. These forms and structures provide great practicality and coherence by revealing causalities in our world. They yield objective truth, though not absolute truth.

The choice is ours: either we define *objectivity* as a pure, direct perception, thus nullifying it and rendering the world unexplainable; or we define *objectivity* as a mediate, verifiable perception, thus rendering it productive and the world explainable. I maintain that the latter is the sane choice.

Hence, I believe that my friend will now agree that Madonna was objectively absent from my class on that day. And I admit to my friend that postmodernism has had some good effects, especially in the arts. Insofar as it has been a Midrash, a loosening of imagination, an avant-gardism, and an exuberance that is not excessive,[29] it has uplifted, beautified, and enlightened. But I doubt that many postmodernists besides my friend will view this balanced position with favor.

Justus Buchler, too, would see objectivity and subjectivity as metaphysical codimensions, as always operating together. On the one hand, he said: "No human product [or judgment] owes its being entirely to its producer or producers: the world of a producer must allow the production, that is, provide the conditions for it."[30] There is thus an objective dimension to all our judgments or products.

On the other hand, Buchler held, there is also a subjective dimension to all our judgments or products; for a product also " 'expresses' an individual's position in the sense that it reflects facts about the individual, for example, the fact of his being bold and confident." Thus, he concluded, "in every product [or judgment] a revelatory and substantive dimension may be found."[31]

I emphasize only that the balance or tension between objectivity and subjectivity shifts constantly and that life meanings, especially, call for an appreciation of both these dimensions—or else one may misdirect one's life and suffer what existential psychoanalysts call "ontological guilt."

Radical postmodernists simulate gods in denying the existence of objectivity because they imply that nothing can restrain their subjectivity or force their life meanings to change. This is a delusion of omnipotence. Religious fundamentalists also simulate gods in claiming to comprehend the word of God perfectly, unmediated by history and their own subjectivity or fallibility. This is a delusion of omniscience.

Religious fundamentalists and radical postmodernists reject basic tenets of modernity, but the former did so much earlier and for a different reason. For example, traditional Judaism introduced during the Enlightenment a virtual "freeze" on the law's dynamism in order to seclude Judaism from modernity's revolutionary challenges. Right-wing Orthodoxy still takes that rigid view of halakhah, of the legal process, still maintains that "freeze" of premodernity's last breath.

Emanuel Rackman describes the "freeze" thus: "Codes which were never intended to be final oracles became more immutable than the Bible, and customs, even forms of dress, which were hardly Jewish in origin, were canonized because they coincided in time with the 'freeze.' "[32]

Pope Pius IX is another and different example of such a religious reactionary. Garry Wills shows how Pius's *Syllabus of Errors* (1864) "plunged . . . into wild charges against 'the modern world,' " condemning, for instance, the idea that, in Pius's words, "every man is free to embrace and profess that religion which, guided by the light of reason, he shall consider true."

Furthermore, Pius planned to block all liberal or modern opposition within the Roman Catholic Church by having the definition of papal infallibility include even ordinary doctrinal statements of the Pope, such as the *Syllabus*. The Vatican Council (1870) limited the definition, however, to those occasions when the Pope speaks ex cathedra regarding faith and morals.[33]

Because many fundamentalists and reactionaries are latent totalitarians, hoping to ban all versions of religion and morality other than their own, they imagine God to be a totalitarian. They feel certain that their version of religion possesses the only true meaning of life—certain enough for some to commit murder or suicide for their life meaning.

Chapter 3

Suicide and Meanings of Life

Our cat, Hogan, has been traveling much since Spider, a stray kitten, moved into our home, and on returning, he frequently lashes out at Spider; but I doubt that Hogan is driven to ponder life's meaning, despite his Irish connection. Such meaning is vital for human beings, however, since its loss or prevalence may induce suicide. What leads some people to kill themselves and what inspires others to go on living are two sides of the same continuum.

My periodontist chatted with me during osseous surgery today. "So, Jerry, are you writing?" I grunted in the affirmative. "What are you writing on?" The nurse sucked out the debris, and I mumbled the title. He stopped grinding and told me this dream. A wise man was speaking to him about the importance of people discovering the meaning of life for themselves.

When Dr. Guild felt himself awakening, he said to the wise man: "Tell me quickly, how do I go on living if I find that life has no meaning?" The dream ended, and the grinding resumed.

I examine Emile Durkheim's century-old sociological study of suicide because it bears strongly on our theme and many social scientists still deem it relevant.[1] He found that "every disturbance of equilibrium [in the social order], even though it achieves greater comfort and a heightening of general vitality, is an impulse to voluntary death." But, he asked, how can that which generally improves life cause suicide?[2] He answered thus:

Happiness, or "even exist[ence]," is only possible if our means sufficiently fulfill or balance our needs. Unsatisfied needs are painful, and thus tend to be unrepeated after a while; eventually, they atrophy. But "as the impulse to live is merely the result of all the rest [of impulses], it is bound to weaken as the others relax." Suicide is the natural consequence when such impuissance becomes pervasive.[3]

Our minds suggest a host of attractive ends far beyond the needs of instinct; indeed, such suggestions have no psychological limit. But actually having countless desires is morbid because pursuing "a goal which is by definition unattainable is to condemn oneself to . . . perpetual unhappiness." Only society can be the moderating force, for it is the "only moral power" whose authority one accepts. "Only conscience" as an organ of society can set a limit to the passions.[4] *"But when society is disturbed by some painful crisis or by beneficent but abrupt transitions, it is momentarily incapable of exercising this influence; thence come the sudden rises in the curve of suicides which we have pointed out above."*[5]

The masses who suffer from a sudden economic depression would do well to reduce their requirements and restrain their needs. Their "moral education" needs to be revised. "But society cannot adjust them instantaneously to this new life and teach them to practice the self-repression to which they are unaccustomed."[6]

Society fails likewise when wealth grows abruptly—when sudden prosperity multiplies desire and overweening ambition makes fulfillment impossible. The standards that had adjusted economic needs crumble, and social forces lose their equilibrium. "The state of de-regulation or *anomy*" is intensified because the passions receive less discipline precisely when they need more discipline.[7]

The fact that poverty is in itself a restraint, Durkheim said, explains the striking immunity to suicide in poor countries. People who are accustomed to lack of power do not increase their needs boundlessly—especially, I should add, before the postmodern revolution in communications. But the power of wealth "deceives us into believing that we depend on ourselves only," and all limitation seems intolerable.[8]

I think that such was Jesus' meaning on saying "it is easier for a camel to pass through the eye of a needle than for a rich man to enter the kingdom of God" (Matthew 19:24): the rich tend to depend only on themselves, even for salvation; but "for men this is impossible, while everything is possible for God" (Matthew 19:26). Simeon b. Zoma, a young talmudic sage, also advised against excessive ambition: "Who is he that is rich? He who rejoices in his lot" (Aboth 4:1). Durkheim did not argue against wealth; he only showed the moral danger of sudden wealth.[9]

He observed at the close of the modern period that in social life only trade and industry were in a chronic state of anomy and that they were constantly among the occupations which had the highest rates of suicide. "For a whole century, economic progress has mainly consisted in freeing industrial relations from all regulation, . . . [from] a whole system of moral forces"—from the influences of religion, government, and business itself.[10]

He noted that "anomy is a regular and specific factor in suicide in our modern societies" and that it occurs in spheres other than industry. For example, matrimonial anomy prevails in divorce and widow-hood, and a parallel rise in suicides occurs during these crises—especially large where law and custom permit an "excessive" practice of divorce. Durkheim categorized suicides resulting from social deregula-tion as *anomic suicide*.[11]

His portrayal of chronic anomy a century ago is even more representative of present society—for now chronic anomy is widespread. "Reality" was then aban-doned for "dreams of fevered imaginations." Greed proliferated "without knowing where to find ultimate foothold." A craving for "novelties, unfamiliar plea-sures, nameless sensations" arose that "in their infinite quantity [could not] form a solid foundation of hap-piness to support one during days of trial."[12] These conditions are much more prevalent in our postmodern society, and hence Durkheim's view of modern society supports those who see postmodernism as beyond modernism rather than as antimodernism.

The twentieth-century revolutions in transporta-tion, communication, war, and medicine have ex-panded and diversified chronic anomy through their great, rapid, and incessant change. We have meta-morphosed genocide as well as genetics, and this is essential to understanding postmodernism. "There is little doubt," Frank Pearce writes in 1989, "that Durkheim's exploration of anomie in *Suicide* is extraordinarily complex and fruitful."[13]

Durkheim noted that only the exceptional person, "the wise man," enjoyed achievements without needing to replace them constantly, and only such persons found in their achievements "an attachment to life in the hour of difficulty." A wise meaning of life rejects the "futility of an endless pursuit."[14]

He implied that anomy begets in most people a weakening or loss of life's meaningfulness because otherwise they would have an "ultimate foothold" or "attachment to life." They are in a state of social disintegration as well as social deregulation: since society no longer provides them with common, stabilizing values, they are thrust into a state of excessive individualism. He did not note this, but anomic suicide is thus connected to egoistic suicide; for he defined the latter as occurring when excessive individualism destroys social integration. Excessive social deregulation and excessive social disintegration are connected.

Talcott Parsons also senses the connection between Durkheim's two types of suicide. He writes that anomic suicide occurs not when the "means" are lacking to accomplish a person's goals, but when these goals cannot be "meaningfully integrated" with the expectations of society's values.[15]

Moreover, Parsons writes, this expressed Durkheim's "great insight that . . . the goals of the individual could not be treated as being independent of the norms and values of the society, but were, in fact, 'given meaning,' that is, legitimized, by these values." This process of internalization, Parsons notes, was also discovered independently in the same period by Freud, Charles H. Cooley, and George H. Mead, and, he adds, this convergence is "one of the great landmarks . . . of modern social science."[16]

Not only does anomic suicide result from a loss or weakening of life's meaning, but so, also, does egoistic suicide. Durkheim held that egoistic suicide "results from man's no longer finding a basis for existence in life,"[17] and I believe that we can faithfully substitute "meaning" for "basis" here.

Durkheim used the category of egoistic suicide to account for the different rates of suicide among Protestants, Catholics, and Jews in nineteenth-century Europe: Protestants killed themselves much more often than Catholics, and still more often than Jews. He based his explanation on the principle that "a religious society cannot exist without a collective credo, and the more extensive the credo the more unified and strong is the society"—and the sturdier is its members' life meaning.[18]

He meant by "credo" more than a statement of religious beliefs; he meant actions as well as ideas. The more numerous these actions and ideas are, the more is "removed from free inquiry" and the more "individual wills converge to one identical goal." Inversely, the more a religious society permits free inquiry and action—the more individualism—the less is society's domination, cohesion, and vitality.

Protestantism was in this sense "less strongly integrated" than Catholicism, and Catholicism was less strongly integrated than Judaism. For "like all *early religions*, [Judaism] consists basically of a body of practices minutely governing all the details of life and leaving little free room to individual judgment."[19]

This portrayal of Judaism reflects more than the Enlightenment's general bias against that which is outside the pale of Reason, such as rites and mysteries. It reflects the Enlightenment's special form of anti-Semitism, for the term "early religions" is a bowdlerized translation of Durkheim's original *les religions inférieures*—inferior religions. He also demeaned "the Jew" as "primitive [*primitif*] in certain respects"[20]; and he left no doubt that *primitif* is here pejorative since it refers to his contemporary Jews. Durkheim, former rabbinic student and a rabbi's son, shared this bias against traditional Judaism also with contemporary liberal and assimilated Jews.

He also saw Christianity's longstanding reproach of the Jews as another cause of their low rates of suicide. It had inspired the Jews to a remarkable solidarity—to form their own compact and coherent societies because they were banned from a free communication with the majority. But Durkheim greatly exaggerated in saying that in these Jewish societies "everyone thought and lived alike."[21]

He saw this cause operating also in Christian societies, but to a lesser degree; for Catholic suicides increased in countries where they were in the majority, and Protestant suicides decreased in countries where they were in the minority. Here, too, the minority confession had to exercise a rigorous self-discipline because of the majority confession's hostility; it had to "practice greater morality."[22] But Jews had to be more self-disciplined than any Christian minority, since they faced the most hostility. Religion and peoplehood were thus essential to Jews as life meanings, for the courage to continue life.

I would add, however, that apart from the above extrinsic cause, a zeal for life meaning has been intrinsic to Judaism since long before the birth of Christianity. Huston Smith considers Judaism's unique and amazing impact on Western civilization to be "one of the greatest puzzles of history," and he suggests that "what lifted the [ancient] Jews from obscurity to permanent religious greatness was their passion for meaning"; and, he observes, they have continued to strive for meaning in God, in creation, in human existence, in history, in morality, in justice, in suffering, and in Messianism. They have "struggle[d] to make sense out of life."[23]

Durkheim found Protestantism's spirit of free inquiry to have been "related" to, but not the "cause" of, its relatively high rates of suicide. Free inquiry is not intrinsically desirable because it involves as much sorrow as happiness; it is caused only by "the overthrow of traditional beliefs." We question the authority of traditional beliefs only after they have lost some of their authority, just as we reflect on habits only after they have become "disorganized." The unsettlement grows until a new system of beliefs acquires the old authority. Suicide and free inquiry have the same cause—the fall of traditional beliefs.[24]

The desire for free inquiry must be accompanied by the desire for learning because knowledge is the only means of achieving free thought's purposes, and the search for such knowledge begins after "irrational beliefs or actions have lost their hold." That is why, for example, "philosophy . . . appears as soon as religion has lost its sway, and only then."[25]

Durkheim thus expected the desire for learning to correspond to the rate of suicide and to be stronger among Protestants than among Catholics. He cited the following statistics to support his thesis: in Catholic countries 66 percent of children aged 6 to 12 years attended school (1860–61, 1874–75, 1877–78), compared to 95 percent of children in Protestant countries; in Prussia the proportion of Catholic students in secondary schools (1875–76) was 50 percent less than that of Protestant students; and among 1,000 Catholics attending schools of every sort in Prussia (1889), an average of 1.3 attended a university, whereas the average was 2.5 for Protestant students attending a university.[26]

The statistics for Jewish students in the previous cases were as follows: they attended elementary schools at least on a par with Protestants; they attended secondary schools about fourteen times as much as Catholics, and seven times as much as Protestants; and among 1,000 Jews attending schools of every sort, an average of sixteen students attended a university—compared to 1.3 for Catholics and 2.5 for Protestants. The Jews were thus a conspicuous exception—they were the most educated and yet had the least suicides.[27]

Durkheim adduced a "general law" for this exception: every religious minority tries to surpass the surrounding population in knowledge in order to protect itself against the majority's hate. Because Jews were the smallest and most-hated minority, they were the most inspired to acquire knowledge. But their learning was not a replacement of faith because their faith was still strong, and knowledge by itself neither weakens a vigorous tradition nor occasions suicide. Jews thus had "all the intelligence of modern man without sharing his despair."[28]

Again, I point to the intrinsic factor, which Durkheim again omitted. The Jewish zeal for education did not arise only from the extrinsic factor of Christian hostility, just as I noted earlier that the Jewish passion for meaning did not arise only from that same extrinsic factor; both propensities had prevailed in Judaism since before Christianity. I made the same point earlier with regard to Freud: he saw our love of beauty originating from an extrinsic factor only, but such love is also intrinsic. We ought not to overlook, or neglect, our intraests in beauty, learning, social integration, and life meanings.

The intrinsic factors are essential; the extrinsic factors cannot by themselves explain these phenomena. For, contrary to Durkheim's "general law," many oppressed minorities have not pursued education. We need to examine intrinsic and extrinsic factors for a fuller understanding, but I think that it is the intrinsic strength of a tradition's value of learning that chiefly determines the prevalence of education. Still, extrinsic factors can over a long period create or destroy a traditional value.

Jews had been studying Torah since the Second Temple Period in order to gain God's reward,[29] in order to know how to do God's bidding,[30] and as a way of being in God's presence.[31] They believed that the study of nature would also reveal God— "The heavens declare the glory of God, and the firmament showeth his handiwork" (Psalm 19:2)— and that wisdom, the integration of experience, knowledge, understanding, and tradition into everyday life, originates in awe—"Awe of God is the beginning of wisdom" (Proverbs 9:10).

Their desire for learning was so deep that it prevailed even after the Enlightenment and Emancipation had weakened or cut education's link to God for most Western European Jews.[32] Learning was a way of life for Jews when Durkheim wrote, inherently opposed to suicide; it was a way of fulfillment and not merely a defensive measure.[33] Even now, an assimilating century after Durkheim, in the United

States the proportion of Jewish students and professors in higher education significantly exceeds the proportion of Jews in the population.

Let us, however, remember Durkheim's main point about egoistic suicide: its cause is intrinsic to the community because it is an act of rootlessness that arises from the disintegration of the community's meaning of life. Parsons considers this point still valid, but "largely for ideological reasons, this basic insight is still far from being fully assimilated into the thinking of social scientists."[34]

The idea that balance is a vital need in social as well as biological phenomena is basic in Durkheim's thought. All of his categories of suicide entail extremes in either social regulation or social integration. Just as egoistic suicide results from "excessive individuation," so altruistic suicide results from "insufficient individuation." Altruistic suicide occurs "when social integration is too strong"—when "the goal of conduct is exterior to itself [the ego], that is, [the goal is] in one of the groups in which it participates."[35]

Note that the preceding etiologies of *egoistic* and *altruistic* suicide are without moral connotation. They return to root meanings, to a time before the ever-spreading invasion of morality into descriptive language reached these words. *Egoistic* does not mean here "selfish," and *altruistic* does not mean here "unselfish"—as they do in present ordinary usage. They refer here only to the ego's degree of agency, and they do not prejudge the morality of their diverse and complex manifestations.[36]

Yet the words Durkheim used in applying his value-free etiologies are biased—to our ears, anyhow. Thus, he considered *obligatory suicide*, one of three varieties of altruistic suicide, to be caused by society's making suicide a duty in some circumstance; for example, on one's becoming sick or old or widowed. Durkheim cited a page and half of such examples, but all of them, he said, occurred among "primitive peoples" or in "lower societies."[37]

Still, these biased terms contain the anticipation of a great anthropological insight. Durkheim's "primitive peoples" correspond to those people who lived before the Axial Age as Karl Jaspers later marked it. Jaspers noted that they had a mythical view of the cosmos, an organic relation to society, and they followed society's norms automatically or unquestioningly, including suicide norms and life meanings. But the consciousness of individuality with its questioning attitude, Jaspers observed, first arose in the Axial Age (800–200 B.C.E.), and that is when, I argue, the meaning of life first emerged as a problem.

Optional suicide, the second variety of altruistic suicide, is also "associated with . . . lower societies" [*des societes inférieures*]. Here, public opinion is "favorable" to suicide in certain circumstances rather than "formally requiring" it; it is done to "win esteem" rather than to "escape the stigma of insult." Durkheim offered a paragraph of examples. He admitted, however, that the optional and obligatory varieties are so closely related that "it is impossible to distinguish where one begins and the other ends."[38]

I conjecture that optional suicide originated at the beginning of the Axial Age, when the transition toward a consciousness of individuality began. The old obligational authority of society's suicide norms had begun to weaken, leaving a small space for personal options. During this transitional period the question of life's meaning first flitted through a few minds, although one cannot say about a succession of historical ages exactly where one begins and the other ends.

Acute suicide, the third variety of altruistic suicide, differs from the others in not requiring any special circumstance; it is done for the sake of "renunciation itself." Durkheim's examples were mostly from India, and he noted that in every case the person sought "to strip himself of his personal being in order to be engulfed in something which he regards as his true essence." Impersonality is here acute.[39]

Jaspers viewed the middle of the Axial Age, around the sixth century B.C.E., as "the most crucial turning point in history" because "it was then that man as he is today was born," that consciousness of individuality came of age.[40] And it was then, he noted, that the following religions were created—in response, I argue, to the question of life's meaning, which had by then become a problem for many. The religions were those of Confucius (551?–479? B.C.E.), Lao-tse (604?–? B.C.E.), Upanishads (sixth century B.C.E.), Buddha (563?–483? B.C.E.), Zoroaster (sixth or seventh century B.C.E.), and, I would add, the Deuteronomic worldview as articulated in Jeremiah's prophetic revolution in Judaism (seventh–sixth centuries B.C.E.).

Jeremiah, who began to prophesy in 627 B.C.E., preached a meaning of life that confirmed individuality. He could argue with God (Jeremiah 12:1): "Right wouldest Thou be, O Lord, were I to contend with Thee, yet will I reason with Thee: wherefore doth the way of the wicked prosper, and wherefore are all they secure that deal very treacherously?" H. Freedman notes in the Soncino's edition of Jeremiah: "It is apparently the first time that [this] problem is raised in the Bible."

Armand Abecassis observes that whereas the "classical prophets had, above all, insisted on the salvation of the people, as such, and on its collective identity, with Jeremiah there was a deepening of the personal and human aspects, and emphasizing of these aspects within the social and natural order."[41] And Marc-Alain Ouaknin adds: "This deepening was not the invention of selfishness but the understanding of man as a separate and unique being."[42]

For Buddha, however, escape from individuality was the meaning of life. *Nirvana* was his name for life's ultimate goal, life's meaning. Huston Smith notes that the word's etymology refers to an intransitive "extinguishment," as in a fire that goes out when deprived of fuel. Nirvana is a state where all "the boundaries of the finite self," of individuality and its problems, have been extinguished—where private desire and consciousness have been entirely consumed and where "boundless life itself" prevails. It is a state, Buddha said, that is "incomprehensible, indescribable, inconceivable, unutterable."[43] The other religions responded to the alienation with different meanings of life.

The intellectual factor of acute suicide may lie in a corruption of Buddha's concept of nirvana. For Durkheim viewed the acute suicide as seeking "to strip himself of his personal being in order to be engulfed in something which he regards as his true essence." I say *corruption* because, for Buddha, suicide could not bring about the supreme state. Yet note that most of Durkheim's examples of acute suicide were from India, Buddha's country and first sphere of great influence.

Altruistic suicide and egoistic suicide are thus at opposite poles of the same continuum—that of individuation or, from the reverse perspective, that of social integration. Altruistic suicide "disregards everything relating solely to the individual," while egoistic suicide "sets human personality on so high a pedestal that it can no longer be subordinated to anything." Durkheim's bias emerged again in application; for he deemed altruistic suicide to be related to a "crude morality" (*rude morale*), and egoistic suicide to be closely associated with a "refined ethics" (*éthique raffinée*).[44]

Still, Durkheim said also that altruistic suicide had occurred in "more recent civilizations"—by implication, in those with a "refined ethics"—notably, among Christian martyrs. Their enthusiastic embracement of death showed that they had then "completely discarded their personalities" for the sake of an ideal. They chose death, though their hands did not do the deed; they had knowingly behaved so as to bring on death. Durkheim considered this to be suicide, which he defined as follows: "To be suicide, the act [whether active or passive] from which death must necessarily result need only have been performed by the victim with full knowledge of the facts."[45]

I agree that voluntary martyrdom and acute suicide are somewhat similar: both involve a "stripping of personal being" for the sake of an ideal. Neither suicide was possible much before the Axial Age because both pertain to people who were conscious of their individuality. But I argue that acute suicide applies to those with the weak consciousness of individuality, which typifies the transition to the Axial Age, whereas martyrdom often entails the strong consciousness of individuality and life meaning, which arose only after history's "turning point." The latter fully know that to be untrue to their life's meaning would entail a pointless, unbalanced, and self-reproachful life.

Some reject Durkheim's definition of *suicide* because it includes martyrdom, because it is free of moral judgment. They consider martyrdom saintly and suicide immoral. The two concepts are disparate, they say, and should be kept apart. They think that such logical cohabitation leads to maculate conceptions, to offspring born in sin. Yet it was precisely because these concepts are logically affiliated that late Latin and late Greek Church writings introduced the Greek word *martyr*, meaning "a witness" to the faith. They thus distinguished noble suicide from sinful suicide, but each is logically a suicide.

Secularists have used the same gambit for their heroes, sacrificing logic for moral advantage. Thus, when I called the death of Plato's Socrates a *suicide*,[46] in the logical sense, some scholars objected; they could see him only as a martyr to Truth. Yet he chose to die and that is logically an act of suicide. Voluntary martyrdom is a useful concept and word because it ennobles passive resistance; but, for knowledge to advance, we must temporarily push back morality's invasion of the word and find the concept camouflaged in suicide. We should first view it objectively, and then judge it morally.

Euthanasia's active and passive ways, too, whatever their religious or moral values, are all acts of killing. We should fully face the act as well as the circumstances. Such objectivity is as much a requirement for moral and legal judgments as it is for the advancement of knowledge. But fundamentalists, who quote text and ignore context, focus on euthanasia's act and blink at voluntary martyrdom's act, while the tender minded blink at both acts. Ultimately, the fundamentalists and the tender minded view these subjects differently because of their different meanings of life.

Durkheim gave the opposite of anomic suicide on the social regulation continuum only a footnote, although he granted chapters to egoistic, altruistic, and anomic suicides. He thought that dwelling on it was useless because it had "so little contemporary importance." He called it *fatalistic suicide*, and he defined it as "the suicide deriving from excessive regulation, that of persons with futures pitilessly blocked and passions violently choked by oppressive discipline." Perhaps it had "historical interest," as in the frequent suicides of "slaves" or others under "excessive physical or moral despotism," but such conditions, he believed, hardly existed in his day.[47]

Actually, life on the social regulation continuum was not so free of fatalism then, and it warranted at least a chapter, but who could say today what Durkheim said in 1897? After a century in which untold millions were tortured and murdered by German Nazis, Russian and Chinese communists, and African dictatorships, numbers of victims never before approximated, who could now think that excessive despotism seldom happens—or that civilization is progressing morally? The twentieth century is characterized as much by fatalism as by anomy and egoism.

Indeed, the rates of suicide and suicide attempts rose sharply as the twentieth century progressed. Kay Redfield Jamison reports in 1999:

> Suicide in the young, which has tripled over the past forty-five years, is, without argument, one of our most serious public health problems. Suicide is the third leading cause of death in young people in the United States and the second for college students. The 1995 National College Health Risk Behavior Survey, conducted by the Centers for

Disease Control and Prevention, found that one in ten college students had seriously considered suicide during the year prior to the survey; most had gone so far as to draw up a plan.

The figures for high school students surveyed in 1997 are even more worrying. One in five high school students said he or she had seriously considered suicide during the preceding year, and most of them had drawn up a suicide plan. Nearly one student in ten actually attempted suicide during the twelve-month period. One out of three of the suicide attempts was serious enough to require medical attention. . . .

Myrna Weissman, a psychiatric epidemiologist at Columbia University in New York, has found compelling evidence of a dramatic doubling or even tripling of rates of suicide attempts [in general] over recent decades. . . . [48]

From Jamison's psychological viewpoint, the rates of suicide would be most diminished by a reduction in the number of clinical depressions; while from Durkheim's sociological viewpoint, the rates of suicide would be most diminished by a society's approach to the middles of the social regulation and social integration continua because the axes of a satisfactory life lie there. I believe that these views are complementary. Durkheim would see a happy union of love of neighbor and love of self, for example, as being near equipoise on the social integration continuum.

Life at the middle, on the balance, of the social regulation continuum is equally important for promoting civil and personal welfare, and thus obviating suicide. But this is equally difficult to achieve. For example, *Newsweek* concluded in 1996 with regard to civil welfare that "in today's environmental debates, the moderate and reasonable center has become a dangerous place to be."[49] That is also true of the public debate on abortion. The "center" to which *Newsweek* referred is that of the social regulation continuum—between anomy and fatalism.

Finding the middle of these continua in social and personal life is difficult because the matter is very complex. First, the various manifestations of a continuum have each movable axes. Each axis's location pertains to a particular situation, and determining its location depends on a complex of chance, reason, feeling, intuition, and experience.

For example, legislation of speech is one manifestation on the social regulation continuum, and its axis moves according to the situation—whether that is peace or war, libel or testimony, biography or pornography, or falsely shouting "fire" in a crowded or uncrowded theater. Locating a satisfactory axis of the situation is often difficult, and it is even more difficult in marginal situations—such as a cold war.

Moreover, every situation involves more than one continuum, and all of the continua need to be coordinated with each other. For example, each of the various situations of abortion entails the social regulation and social integration continua, and an axis of legislation needs to be coordinated with an axis of the mother's individualism. A situation's balance often requires that one or more of its continua's axes be at the extreme, not at the middle. For instance, extremism in many continua is required in defense of a nation's imperiled freedom, as Barry Goldwater argued. We never have the luxury of balancing a single, isolated continuum because we are always in a situation.

Finally, because life meanings are formed by particular social and personal situations, a new situation might challenge them. Some would be afraid to recognize the new situation's suitable balance because it threatens their usual equilibrium. Others would find situations such as the Holocaust or an epiphany conversional and change their life's meaning. Fanatics are blind to a situation's implications for such change, most people blink at them, and a few bravely risk disequilibrium and look into them.

Durkheim emphasized the temporal and causal primacy of social experience over "abstract ideas," and thus, by implication, over meanings of life. "Religious conceptions are the products of the social environment," he said, "rather than its producers," and these ideas can modify this environment only superficially. We can "conceive of the world"—hence, the meaning of life—"only in the image of [our] small social world."[50] He recognized, however, that a social world can change radically over a long time— for instance, from altruism to egoism—and thus cause radical changes in religious ideas or life meanings.

This account has much truth, but I disagree with its absolute unilateralism. It overlooks the ability of geniuses to transcend important aspects of their era, and it omits the ability of charismatic leaders to generate deep changes in the social world. It disregards the power of a mind or personality conscious of its individuality. A few individuals have initiated great ideas and significant social change.

Such individualistic minds did not exist before the Axial Age, and the question of life's meaning did not arise in minds unconscious of individual agency. They sensed life as an organic unity with the cosmos. Their ideas, feelings, values, and life meanings were experienced as organic elements of the world. The question of life's meaning arose amorphously when the dim morning star light of individuality first shone and evoked an inchoate, fearful sense of separation from the world: Who am I? Who are they? Where are we? What should I do? Self and other are polarities on the same continuum, and perceptions of them originated together.[51]

Life's meaning became a persistent problem only with the light of dawn, with the crucial turn from a vague sense of individuality to a clear consciousness of personal agency. But persons also felt the world's awesomeness and their own limitations; they encountered the abyss and sought salvation; they became conscious of consciousness, and they thought about thought; they examined and rejected opinions, customs, and conditions that had never been questioned; they followed *logos* rather than *mythos* and produced the basic categories that still frame our thought.[52]

Even more striking, this momentous turn occurred almost simultaneously in China, India, and the West, as is evidenced by the philosophies and religions they then created; and yet none of these civilizations was aware of the others. But what brought about this independent, widespread, and simultaneous crucial turn? Jaspers could say only that "the fact of the threefold axial age is a kind of miracle, in the sense that any really adequate explanation lies beyond our present scientific horizon."[53]

Jaspers observed that the long epoch's development was not a straight climb. Its discovery of what was later to be called "reason and personality" was made by a few, but the crowd could not follow. The mythical spirit receded imperceptibly as the crowd's background of life, and so it triumphed again and

again. But humanity ultimately took the leap forward, and what began as freedom of movement ended
as anarchy—or anomy—in all three regions, and an
urge to restore stability grew out of the intolerable
disorder.[54]

> And the Children of Israel said unto Moses and
> Aaron: "Would that we had died by the hand of
> the LORD in the land of Egypt, when we sat by
> the flesh-pots, when we did eat bread to the full;
> for ye have brought us forth into this wilder-
> ness, to kill this whole assembly with hunger."
> (Exodus 16:3)

You will recall that Huston Smith considers
Judaism's unique and immense impact on Western
civilization to be one of history's "greatest puzzles,"
and he suggests that "what lifted the [ancient] Jews
from obscurity to permanent religious greatness was
their passion for meaning," and that their "real
impact . . . lies in the extent to which Western civilization took over their angle of vision on the deepest
questions life poses."[55] We can now understand what
inspired this passion for meaning: it was the ancient
Jewish turn to consciousness of personal being and
power—of individuality and freedom.

Robert M. Seltzer observes that biblical religion
"emphasized human and divine freedom to an unprecedented extent," that it rejected the pagan idea
of "a primordial, inescapable Fate to which man
and gods are subject." Indeed, the Jewish Bible's
overarching theme seems to be that of "the tension
between God's will and man's."[56] Such tension can
exist only between those who are acutely conscious
of their individuality.

Harold Bloom imagines a woman to have been the author of "The Book of J," which secular scholarship views as the oldest strand in the Bible; and he conjectures that she was at Solomon's court in the tenth century B.C.E. He sees her main interest to have been "the elite image of the *individual* life," and he considers her to have been "the greatest of all ironists."[57] Only one who has a personal identity can be ironic. If Bloom is right, then the ancient Jews attained consciousness of individuality at least a century before Jaspers's dating of the Axial Age.

I sense the dramatic emergence of the individual in the Torah's following account. God instructs Moses to approach Pharaoh for the deliverance of the Israelites, but Moses says, "Who am I" to do these things? Plainly, Moses is presented as modest, but I hear also a faint cry in the morning star light, "who am I?"

God tries to assure Moses, but he remains uneasy. What shall he tell the Children of Israel is the name of the God who has sent him to them? "And God said unto Moses: 'I AM THAT I AM'; and He said: 'Thus shalt thou say unto the Children of Israel—I AM hath sent me unto you'" (Exodus 3:10–14). This is a name of sheer personhood and utter individuality; this God does not submit to Fate.

Moreover, this was a new name, for a new perception. It pertains to YHVH—indeed, Maimonides considered them to be the same name[58]—of which God said to Moses: "I appeared unto Abraham, unto Isaac, and unto Jacob as God Almighty, but by My name YHVH I was not known to them" (Exodus 6:3). A new consciousness of God's nature emerged here. Moses declared: "Hear O Israel—YHVH our God, YHVH is One" (Deut. 6:4). I think that "One" means *Singular*, and this excludes pantheism as well as polytheism. The ancient Jews became increasingly conscious of personal being.

That is why they valued the right to privacy. Emanuel Rackman writes that "even in ancient Judaism no attempt was ever made to invade the privacy of Jews by ferreting out information as to what they believed or how they behaved [privately]." For example, the Torah left male and female on their honor upon becoming ritually unclean to count, "for himself" and "for herself," the number of clean days before undergoing ritual immersion in water and becoming ritually clean again; and there was no outside supervision.[59] Only those who feel personal identity can have the idea of privacy.

But the question persists: How did the ancient Israelites arrive at this critical stage of consciousness? Jaspers could not explain it, and the postulate that it was divinely inspired also leaves us with a mystery. Durkheim's principle, that only a momentous change in social reality can explain such a momentous development, offers some hope of an answer. But what was that change?

Intriguingly, the Torah relates such a momentous change in the Israelites' social reality: the change from a generation of slaves in Egyptian cities to a generation born free and wandering in the desert. But we have no historical or archaeological evidence of the Exodus.

Still, I have a piquant sense that the Torah's cryptic mention of "a mixed multitude" who joined the Israelites in the Exodus (Exodus 12:38) holds a clue to such a momentous social change. The "multitude" is not identified; no reason is given for its joining, and it is never mentioned again.

Jaspers's essay may also contain a clue. He noted similarities of changing social conditions in the three regions of the Axial Age: an astonishing (abrupt?) prosperity produced by an abundance (a multitude) of small states and cities in constant tension with each other, and a swift intellectual movement created by travel and trade (mixing) within each region.[60] Such a complex might well have been anomic and generated a consciousness of individuality. Perhaps the Torah's "mixed multitude" alludes to a similar complex.

I noted this connection between anomy and individuality earlier with regard to suicide; namely, that anomic suicide is connected to egoistic suicide because excessive social deregulation begets excessive social disintegration. I note now the converse connection: excessive social disintegration begets excessive social deregulation. Excessive individualism begets the breakdown of law and social order, and likewise for the converse. Such causality holds not only between the continua, but also on each continuum: excess leads egoism and anomy respectively to altruism and fatalism, and vice versa. Such has been the whirligig of history ever since the Axial Age.

Durkheim considered "every sort of suicide [as] . . . merely the exaggerated or deflected form of a virtue." Altruism is a sentiment that can induce courage, and egoism is a sentiment that can induce respect for others—because prizing individual personality in oneself as an end can lead to the appreciation of it also in other people. When excessive, however, egoism can induce selfishness, and altruism can induce the sacrifice of another's life as easily as one's own.[61] The "golden rule" requires the "golden mean."

So, we've arrived through yet another route to the ancient wisdom that a contented life, and thus a persevering life, requires a comprehensive balance; and it requires above all else meaning, as Dr. Guild's dream recognized—"How do I go on living if I find that life has no meaning?" But not all meanings support one's life; some lead to metaphorical or literal self-destruction. Egoism, anomy, and other fanaticisms are such self-destructive life meanings. Reason alone cannot validate or invalidate any life meaning; but if we "choose life" over death, contentment over discontentment, then reason, objectivity, and experience have an important bearing on life's meanings.

Still, we should not overlook the existence of chaos and its power to destroy life meanings. The Torah has chaos existing since the beginning of time: "The earth was chaos and void" (Genesis 1:2). This suggests a metaphysics of chaos: chaos still stirs in all existence, and it erupts randomly. Chaos destroys, but it provides also an opportunity to "repair the world."

Joseph B. Soloveitchik, a luminary of Modern Orthodoxy, put the matter this way:

> When God engraved and carved out the world, He did not entirely eradicate the chaos and the void, the deep and the darkness, from the domain of His creation. . . . Now Judaism affirms the principle of creation out of absolute nothingness. . . . All of these "primordial" materials were created in order that they subsist and be located in the world itself. Not for naught did He create them. He created them in order that they may dwell within the cosmos![62]

Norman Lamm, eminent Modern Orthodox rabbi, sees the chaos of the Holocaust and some other periods as *hester panim*, "the hiding of God's face." He writes:

Now, when I say that *Hester Panim* is a period of meaninglessness, I of course do not intend automatically to nullify all meaning in Jewish history. . . . Rather, what I mean is that the *totality* of Jewish history . . . is the highest form of meaning, in that it represents the engagement of man with God; and by "meaning," I intend nothing less than the universal redemptive design of history. However, *within* this process of meaning there exists [in the people's history] a hiatus, . . . a "bubble," in which meaninglessness pervades. . . .[63]

Some Bible scholars do not find the principle of creatio ex nihilo in Genesis, but all see the existence of chaos there. For those of us, however, for whom the "bubbles" have burst the belief in a "redemptive design of history," the question is: How do chaos and uncertainty otherwise affect our meanings of life?

Chapter 4

Uncertainty, Religion, and Meanings of Life

Uncertainty is a principle in the world of physics; but uncertainty inheres also in the domains of biology and of human affairs, and it is, respectively, even more widespread there. Evolution has increased the dimensions of reality, and has thus sequentially enlarged the range of chance as well as the range of regularity. We exist simultaneously in a complex of physical, biological, and human dimensions, and we are subject to all their intrinsic uncertainties. Yet so many people feel certain about the meaning or purpose of life.

Games attract, in part, because their rules are certain. The rules are ultimately stipulated, not discovered. Facts may persuade us to change them, but facts cannot void them. They enwomb us for a while. But games attract also because their course and outcome are chancy. Games thus invite us to venture within their safe, solid framework of rules.

Games are interested when engaged mainly for shelter from contingencies or for respite from obligation, anxiety, or hope. Yet games offer shelter and respite because they are especially suited to intraestedness; they easily envelop us in a playful presentness. It is thus sometimes in our interest to become intraested. The involvement is then interested, while the act is intraested.

Mathematics is the divine intellectual game and ideally suited to intraestedness, as the famous toast at Cambridge University attests: "To pure mathematics. May it never be of any practical use whatsoever." And although mathematics has often been regarded as the standard of rational knowledge to which other sciences should strive, Kurt Gödel proved in 1931 that it cannot be completely and consistently formalized in one system.

His theorem shows that there is an undeterminable formula in any formal system adequate for number theory—a formula that is not provable and whose negation is not provable. All such systems must be incomplete. A corollary shows that the consistency of such systems also cannot be proved within the system. Even Ralph Waldo Emerson would have admitted that consistency is essential to mathematics, that it is not the "hobgoblin" of small-minded mathematicians. Thus, even in the sphere under our strictest control there is constituent incompleteness and undecidability—i.e., intrinsic uncertainty. How much more so in all other spheres!

Yet countless people believe in the certainty of religion and its meaning of life, a sphere rife with doubt and controversy. Many confuse certitude, a feeling of certainty, with objective certainty, since doubt and ambiguity of religious fundamentals frighten them. They need to believe in religious inerrancy, or moral infallibility, or fixed cosmic purpose, or perennial philosophy. These beliefs are for many at the center of life's meaning.

I focus in this chapter on Orthodox Judaism, but similar considerations apply also to branches of Christianity and Islam. The Orthodox are my imagined interlocutors because they claim certainty over more religious issues than do the adherents of Judaism's other branches. Hence, I use traditional readings of traditional sources in my arguments and not the "unkosher" readings of secular scholarship. For example, for the sake of argument I accept uncritically the Talmud's attribution of views to particular rabbis even where secular scholarship finds otherwise.

I begin with Eliezer Berkovits, a Modern Orthodox rabbi who uses a familiar argument against the view that existence has no meaning or value apart from those we give it. He contends that if "the only meanings, the only values, are those created by man," then "which man's?" Which of contrary values should we adopt, since none can be wrong? Indeed, "if carried to its logical conclusion," such subjectivity "leads to a justification of nazism itself." He concludes, therefore, that our only solution, our only way of attaining objective certainty, is by a "reference to the transcendental [God] for values [or meaning]."[1]

How striking that this obviously false and invalid conclusion is accepted by so many! For even religions that center on a transcendental personal God disagree on salvation, morality, and life meanings; for instance, on the salvation of non-Christians, on abortion, and on *tikkun ha'olam*, whether our purpose in life is to help God repair this world. Even branches of the same religion disagree thus. Since each claims transcendental authority, the question remains: Whose religious life meanings should we adopt? The transcendentalists can no more avoid subjectivity and uncertainty than can those who deny transcendental meaning.

Furthermore, not all of the Torah's words have been understood, though traditional Jews have for millennia taken its words as God's own. Adin Steinsaltz, the Orthodox talmudic scholar and translator, notes that the evolution of language required an oral tradition to explain some words in the Written Law even when Hebrew was the everyday language. Yet some such words had no oral tradition, and Jewish scholars had "to admit relatively early that [these] words in the Torah . . . were unknown to them . . . ."[2] They are still unknown. "Reference to the transcendental" cannot bring certainty where the Transcendental's words are not grasped.

Even more to the point, Emanuel Rackman differs with Berkovits, although both are Modern Orthodox rabbis. He writes:

> Notwithstanding popular opinion to the contrary, Judaism does not give its adherents unequivocal answers to the basic questions of life. Nor does it . . . prescribe for every situation. . . . While it does have religious, philosophical and ethical imperatives, these are often antithetical . . . and man is rarely spared the onus of deliberate choice and decision. . . .[3]

Rackman sees that all meanings of life, all responses "to the basic questions of life," are ultimately, ontologically, personal choices, and he faces the existential risk; but Berkovits hides his face from the risk, from the subjectivity of his own choices.

Rackman believes in divine revelation, but he recognizes that it is "limited in word and scope." Revelation requires chary interpretations because situations are "complicated, nuanced, and . . . endlessly diverse." Does the prohibition of murder apply in battle to the killing of one's enemies? To enemy captives? To countless other war situations? Thus, "man retains a creative role in the very process of applying revelation," even of the Decalogue. A fortiori, he argues, "one can anticipate an uncertainty or ambiguity" in the rest of revealed Law.[4]

But the majority of the Orthodox community is opposed to Rackman's view. It considers the rabbinic applications of revelation to be absolutely true because they are part of the Oral Law that God gave to Moses on Mt. Sinai together with the Written Law, and which had been passed down orally through the generations. This view claims the clarity and certainty of changelessness, and it is one traditional response. A rabbi put it this way in the Jerusalem Talmud: "Even that which a conscientious disciple later teaches in the presence of his master was already said to Moses on Sinai" (TJ, Pe'ah 2:6, 17a).

This is, however, a foggy view. For, as Steinsaltz says: "We know very little of the origins and early development of the oral law, since information on cultural and spiritual life in the First Temple era is generally sparse."[5] Furthermore, because knowledge in this very conservative view is mere remembrance, it is subject to generational forgetfulness—to contrary traditions and to indecision in the absence of tradition. The Talmud reports a case of such indecision. Some Galilean Jews once asked Rabbi Eliezer b.

Hyrcanus for thirty halakhic decisions, but he gave them only some. His explanation was that he had not heard a ruling from his teachers on the others. They asked: "Are all your words only copies of what you have heard?" To which he replied:

> You wished to force me to say something which
> I have not heard from my teachers. But no man
> ever came to the academy before me or departed
> after me, nor did I ever sleep or doze off there.
> Neither did I ever utter secular speech, or say a
> thing in all my life which I did not hear from my
> teachers. (Sukkah 28a)

Because such extreme conservatism could not sustain life in a changing world, basic changes in the Law had to be introduced—but the conservatives maintained that God had provided these "changes" more than a millennium earlier in the Oral Law, that they were not humanly created. Creative change had to appear as being only a continuity with the past.

This is a premodern view of history, and it was respectable until the Enlightenment.[6] René Descartes (1596–1650) still held the metaphysical basis of this view—namely, the "self-evident" principle that "there must at least be as much reality [or perfection] in the efficient and total cause as in its effect; for whence can the effect draw its reality if not from its cause?"[7]

This principle is that of a closed temporal system, for it precludes the later from having "more" reality or perfection than the earlier—whatever degrees of reality or perfection may mean. It entails entropy, decreasing energy and increasing disorder. Were this principle true, then everything would be running down, and nothing under the sun would be original.

But the Enlightenment brought a spirit of skepticism, empiricism, and objectivity to history and to all social and political thought; it was open to originality, to basic change. David Hume (1711–1776) articulated the metaphysical basis of this view, the modern view—namely, "any thing may produce any thing" within the purview of experience and the rules by which causes and effects are judged.[8] The new may thus be "more" real or perfect than the old; that is, it may be a significant improvement or even original.

The new can be also a significant self-improvement. The Enlightenment gazed critically even on itself for the sake of improvement. Mark Hulliung notes that the most ignored of all the critiques of the Enlightenment are those which the "'age of criticism' made of itself," especially in the disputes between Rousseau and the other philosophes, and that these debates became a valuable heritage, "a matter pertaining to the present no less than to the past."[9]

A few critiques of society had occurred already in the Axial Age—just consider Plato's *Republic*. For that Age's epiphany of individuality and the resultant problem of personal life's meaning also raised questions about social life's purpose. But the extensiveness of the Enlightenment's debates was unprecedented because it had the first vision of a "science of man," which invited diverse "scientific" arguments. Moreover, the philosophes enlarged their already substantial literary audience by concretizing their ideas in plays for the theater.[10]

The philosophes regarded the new as better than the old, but Rousseau saw progress as being also regress: "Our souls have been corrupted in proportion to the advancement of our sciences and arts toward perfection." In other respects, though, he saw progress as "so many steps toward the perfection of the individual and toward the decrepitude of the species."[11] So, neither did Rousseau subscribe to the premodern metaphysics of history.

Yet right-wing Orthodoxy still sees halakhic history with premodern eyes. A right-wing Orthodox rabbi of Agudath Israel of America wrote in 1990: "We are proud to continue the legacy passed on by the generation before us in the great chain of Torah transmission back to Sinai. . . . But the tradition they passed down is not a Judaism that is European; it is a Judaism that passed through Europe"[12]—i.e., without significant change.

The rabbi simply ignored history. For instance, Rabbi Gershom ben Judah banned polygamy for northern Jewry in the eleventh century C.E., which, though biblically allowed, had long been waived in practice. Cecil Roth observes that the ban was "intended to adapt Jewish life to the altered conditions which it had come to face in Europe,"[13] specifically in Christendom. Why else ban what the Torah permits and what is no longer practiced?

The rabbi ignored, too, what right-wing Orthodox Rabbi Steinsaltz recognized: "The Jewish custom of inviting a rabbi to conduct the marriage ceremony dates from the late Middle Ages and is partly an imitation of the Christian ceremony." Steinsaltz noted that the custom has "no religious significance" because matrimony is in halakhah essentially a mutual agreement to live as a family and respect the marriage contract. Halakhically, "the act of marriage almost totally lacks sanctity" as far as the couple is concerned.[14] But few other right-wing Orthodox would acknowledge a Christian influence on a Jewish ceremony.

But the rabbis did respond periodically to deep cultural change with judicial and legislative originality, although mostly they explicitly or implicitly depreciated their role as originators. I believe that this self-depreciation was more than humbleness; it came also from a fear of raising uncertainty about halakhah. The following story in the Talmud, told by Rav Judah in the name of Rav, illustrates my point.

Moses ascended on high and found God affixing to the top of some letters in the Torah coronets, three small written strokes in the form of a crown. He asked: "Why are You adding these? Is there, then, something lacking in the Torah?" God replied: "There will arise after many generations a man, Akiva b. Joseph by name, who will expound upon each tittle heaps and heaps of laws." "Lord of the Universe," Moses said, "permit me to see him."

Moses directly found himself in Rabbi Akiva's academy and listened to the discourse on the law. He was ill at ease because he could not follow the argument. Then a student asked: "Master, whence do you know this?" Rabbi Akiva replied: "It is a law given to Moses at Sinai." Moses was comforted. On returning to God, Moses said: "Lord of the Universe, You have such a man and You give the Torah through me!" And God replied: "Be silent, for such is My will" (Men. 29b).

Rav's story portrays Rabbi Akiva as creating new law. God did not interpret the tittle for Moses, so its meaning could not have been transmitted orally through the generations. The law was new to Moses, yet he was comforted by the statement that God had given it to him at Sinai. And the possibility of uncertainty is similarly stilled for many of today's Orthodox Jews when their rabbis repeat Rabbi Akiva's statement. But uncertainty remains.

A sense of great rabbinic power pervades Rav's story, which even seems to patronize Moses. Not only was this law new to Moses, but he, unlike Rabbi Akiva's students, could not follow its underlying argument; yet he was comforted by the law's claim to certainty. Similarly, after a whole pessimistic discourse on life's uncertainties, Ecclesiastes ends with a statement of certainty: "The end of the matter, all having been heard: fear God, and keep His commandments; for this is the whole man." But uncertainty remains.

Actually, though, the story does not patronize Moses. Rav did not mean to suggest that Moses was less intelligent than Rabbi Akiva or Akiva's students, since tradition ranked Moses as the greatest person in almost all respects. Indeed, Rav himself, together with Samuel, said: "Fifty gates of understanding were created in the world, and all but one were given to Moses" (Nedarim 38a).

Rav implies, rather, that people of an earlier era would be unable to comprehend essential components of a later era because of the radical changes that had since occurred in ideas, culture, and events. One must travel a long, winding road with sharp turns and novel scenes before reaching the gate of understanding and applying halakhah. The story's moral is that rabbis in every generation are obliged to travel that road and to be prepared to create original halakhic paths when needed.

Remarkably, Rav's profound insight was an exception to itself. He was one of those rare ones who transcend their Age at a key point. His insight would appear as radically new even a millennium and a half afterward; it would characterize a much later epoch, after ideas, culture, and events had undergone inconceivable changes.[15]

Rav's insight had to wait until the nineteenth century for it to be recognized explicitly. Thus, in 1882 Friedrich Engels criticized the Enlightenment philosophers' idea that "pure and eternal reason" could be understood and applied to all social problems regardless of the epoch. The philosophes believed, he said, that an "individual man of genius" might have "spared humanity five hundred years of error, strife and suffering" had the genius been born five hundred years earlier. To which Engels remarked: "The great thinkers of the eighteenth century could, no more than their predecessors, go beyond the limits imposed upon them by their epoch."[16] For Rav, even Moses had such limits.

Rav expected future radical changes in culture to occur and to require creative religious responses, as had happened in the millennium and a half since Moses. The halakhah would have to incorporate such historical change for the sake of Judaism's survival. But the halakhah would have to be connected also to its past for the sake of Judaism's identity—even if the connections were fanciful or midrashic, as in claiming a Sinaitic origin. Those who approach halakhah in this way trust their judgment while knowing that certainty about God's truth is unattainable. This road is not for the fainthearted.

Rav's story can be seen also to support his own independent halakhic judgments. His life (third century C.E..), work (cofounder of the Babylonian Talmud), and authority straddled the *tannaitic* and *amoraitic* periods. He was a first-generation *amora*, but he had also been a member of Judah ha-Nasi's law court, the *tanna* who had redacted the Mishnah. He was the only *amora* who had the authority to differ from a *tanna* without basing his view on that of another *tanna*. That is the Talmud's meaning of, "Rav is a *tanna* and differs" (Ket. 8a).

It was Rav's position on rabbinic creativity, not Rabbi Eliezer's, which characterized the halakhic process,[17] even though Rav's underlying reason, his implied sociohistorical premise, was either unrecognized or unacknowledged. The rabbis based the authority for their creativity, instead, on legal grounds, deriving it from the following biblical passage:

> When a legal matter too hard for judgment . . . will arise within your gates, go up to the place that the Lord your God has chosen, and come to the levitical priests and to the judge who will be in those days. Inquire of them, and they will give you the judgment. Act according to their sentence, . . . do all that they instruct you, . . . and do not deviate from what they tell you either to the right or to the left. (Deut. 17:8–11)

Somehow, the rabbis later read this passage in a way that denied halakhic authority to the priests as a body, and that affirmed their own exclusive authority. They interpreted this biblical passage as giving themselves the exclusive right to interpret the Bible halakhically. But how did the rabbis get the exclusive halakhic right to interpret *this* biblical passage?!

Such circular reading dizzies reason and staggers trust; it was a political power play. It served also for many, laity and rabbis, as an a priori buffer against cultural challenges to their halakhic interpretations and life meanings. Like the a priori rules of games, this rabbinic a priori rule cannot be voided by facts; but, as with games, facts may persuade us to abandon the a priori rule.

Rashi (1040–1105 C.E.) read the passage's last clause, "do not deviate to the right or to the left," in a way that extended rabbinic authority to a perturbing extreme. Rashi said that the judge's decision should always be accepted, "even if he decides that right is left and left is right, and surely if he decides that right is right and left is left." The Jerusalem Talmud, however, says only "about the right that it is right and the left that it is left" (Horayot 1:1, 45d).

What perturbs in Rashi's reading becomes more explicit in Nahmanides (1194–1270 C.E.), whose *Commentary* on the Torah adopts Rashi's reading:

> Even if you think that they [the judge and the priests] are wrong, and the matter is as plain as the distinction between your right and left hands, do as they command. Do not ask, "How shall I eat this completely forbidden fat?" or "How shall I execute this innocent man?" Say rather: "God gave me the Torah to be obeyed . . . according to their understanding, even if they are mistaken."

Differences in the gravity of sins or humanistic values do not matter here. One must simply obey the judge, whether to eat forbidden fat or to execute an innocent person, it does not matter which. This reading is fraught with injustice and peril, yet it prevailed over the humanistic characters of Rashi and Nahmanides because it was tied to a life meaning even more important to them, namely, the Law's stability. They believed that rigid obedience to judicial decisions, even to erroneous ones, coheres with God's providence. After all, Rashi and Nahmanides were rabbinic judges.

There are thus opposite positions in Orthodoxy on the scope of rabbinic authority to judge and create law, represented here by Rabbi Eliezer and Rav, and this alone makes Orthodox stands less than certain. The situation calls for halakhic modesty, but few hear the call.

Right-wing Orthodoxy, like Christian fundamentalism, maintains that radical cultural or historical changes pose no challenge to religious doctrine and practice; yet it fears that the faithful would question religious belief through contact with the liberal arts, which are imbued with the modern historical spirit. Hence, right-wing Orthodoxy has generally disapproved of its members acquiring a liberal arts education.

Yet long before the Enlightenment, Louis Jacobs writes, "from the days of Maimonides [1135–1204], there have been [among the rabbis] opponents of all secular learning as well as advocates of it as an aid to faith." Even in his Code of Law, the *Mishneh Torah*, revered by all of Orthodoxy, Maimonides wrote: "the arts and sciences, which reveal the Creator, . . . must be studied with devotion, to one's fullest capacity" ("Laws of Repentance," 10:6).

Hence, Jacobs notes, "the Hasidic teachers were obviously embarrassed by Maimonides's study of secular sciences" since all of them came down "heavily against all secular learning." Rebbe Nahman of Bratzlav (1772–1811) even "dared to criticize Maimonides for his philosophical learnings, not an uncourageous thing to do in his age."[18]

Modern Orthodoxy, however, whose origin moved simple Orthodoxy into the right wing, has adapted itself to the modern view of history; but, being Orthodox as well as modern, it has required support from Jewish traditions different from Rabbi Eliezer's—such as Rav's. There is also a supporting mystical tradition, which sees God and humans as partners in a continuing creation of mystical Torah and "upper worlds."

For example, we find the following in the *Zohar* (thirteenth century):

> IN THE BEGINNING (Genesis 1:1) Rabbi Simeon began by quoting, *I have put My words in your mouth* . . . (Isaiah 51:16). He explained: One should endeavor to study Torah day and night; because the Holy One, blessed be He, listens to the voice of those who study Torah, and a new heaven is created through every new interpretation of the Torah made by them. We learn that as soon as a new interpretation of the Torah leaves a person's mouth it ascends and is presented to the Holy One, blessed be He, and He receives it, kisses it, and adorns it with seventy engraved crowns. . . . [Genesis 4b–5a]

Modern Orthodoxy can draw support, too, from the Jewish humanistic tradition, of which Hillel (c. 60 B.C.E.–10 C.E.) appears as the model.[19] He introduced a system of Torah interpretation that produced new teachings, which he used for the sake of *tikkun ha'olam*, for the commonweal (Mishnah, Gittin 4:3). His creative halakhah helped the underprivileged in several ways.

The mishnaic rabbis also enacted a series of laws for the sake of *tikkun ha'olam*, for the sake of repairing the harm done by previous laws. Some of their repair dealt with divorce, and their purpose was to prevent harm to the wife and the children of her next marriage (Mishnah, Gittin 4:2,3). Other laws were designed to prevent harm to bondmen (Ibid., 4:4,5). Still other laws were created for the sake of *darkhai shalom*, as "ways of peace"; for instance, to permit also the non-Jewish poor to gather *gleanings*, the *forgotten sheaf*, and the *field-corner* (*Ibid.*, 5:8). All of these new laws were inspired by a religious humanism.

This ancient tradition was conspicuous in the shelter of the Jewish homeland; it was noticeable even within the closure of the Diaspora's ghettos; but the Orthodox burrowed it when the Enlightenment shined on them in strange, open places. One hopes against hope that contemporary modern Orthodox rabbis will become courageous enough to follow Rabbi Rackman's lonely lead in allowing the humanistic tradition to emerge from the underground and repair the halakhic cruelty being done to *agunot*.

Rackman recently instituted a rabbinic court to free *agunot* from the halakhic chains that prevent these women from remarrying. It has liberated dozens of them, citing only halakhic sources, but it has "incurred the wrath of Orthodox rabbis from Jamaica Estates to Jerusalem." Rackman writes sadly but unapologetically: "While I have had the support of the Jewish laity, male and female, I have broken ranks with almost all Orthodox rabbis, even with those who are considered to be Modern."[20]

The tradition of humanistic innovation is thus found in halakhah as well as in Jewish mysticism, and it is also present in Jewish philosophy.

Maimonides is not only an exemplar of the humanistic tradition in Jewish philosophy, but he was the first to make explicit, develop, and apply the sociohistorical principle that is implicit in Rav's story, and this principle is a metaphysical basis for Maimonides's humanism. His recognition that human understanding evolves gradually in history was central in his view of religion.

For example, he saw that a sudden abandonment of animal sacrifice as a "way of life" in the Mosaic age would have been similar to a prophet saying in his day: "Your worship should consist solely in meditation without any works at all" because "God has given you a Law forbidding you to pray to Him, to fast, to call upon Him for help in misfortune."[21] The people were not ready in biblical times to abandon animal sacrifice, and Orthodox Jews still pray, today, for the reinstitution of animal sacrifice in a restored Temple of Holiness!

Maimonides believed that since the sacrifice of living beings to idols in temples had been a universal mode of worship in biblical times, God had suffered some of these rites to remain; "but [He] transferred them from created or imaginary and unreal things to His own name, . . . to practice them with regard to Him." Weaning was and is essential, "for a sudden transition from one opposite to another is impossible" because "man, according to his nature, is not capable of abandoning suddenly all to which he was accustomed."[22]

The worship that was sacrifice for a millennium at the Temple of Holiness had "pertain[ed] to [God's] second intention," Maimonides said, "whereas invocation, prayer, and similar . . . modes of worship come closer to [God's] first intention and are necessary for its achievement." Prayer comes "closer" to God's primary intention, but does not reach it; only intraested love (knowledge) of God reaches it, and that is the ultimate meaning of life. Hence, the "people are frequently blamed in the books of the prophets because of their zeal for sacrifices, and it is explained to them that [the sacrifices] are not the object of a purpose sought for its own sake and that God can dispense with them."[23]

Thus, the aim of ritual sacrifices was to bring a primitive people distantly closer to the ideal worship, and Maimonides knew that it would take an eon of gradual human development before the ideal could be approached. Hence, he implied, rabbis should be sensitive to the cultural and historical changes that affect this development in order to achieve halakhah's goal—namely, to bring the people to a closer realization of God's primary intention by revising, repealing, and devising laws of the second intention. God and humans are partners in this "teleological" process, which Rackman calls "the only authentic Halachik approach."[24]

Seven times Maimonides called the Torah's implicit gradualism a "gracious" or "divine ruse." For instance, he said: "Through this divine ruse [i.e., the biblical rites of animal sacrifice] it came about that the memory of *idolatry* was effaced and that the grandest and true foundation of our belief— namely, the existence and oneness of the deity—was firmly established. . . ." He said the same about the biblical "promises [of rewards] and threats [of punishments] with regard to the whole Law"; namely, that "this too is a ruse used by Him with regard to us in order to achieve His first intention with respect to us."[25]

Maimonides said to the one or two contemporaries who might understand his cryptic book:

I know that on thinking about this [divine ruses] at first your soul will necessarily have a feeling of repugnance toward this notion and will feel aggrieved because of it; and you will ask me in your heart and say to me: How is it possible that none of the commandments, prohibitions, and great actions . . . should be intended for its own sake, but . . . invented for our benefit by God in order to achieve His first intention? What was to prevent Him, may He be exalted, from revealing His first intention and from procuring us the capacity to accept this? In this way there would have been no need for the things that you consider to be due to a second intention [i.e., for ruses].[26]

Maimonides answered his imaginary interlocutor: "God does not change at all the nature of human individuals by means of miracles."[27] God had intended to add a unique species to Creation—human beings: beings whose special understanding evolves; beings for whom uncertainty is inescapable and an opportunity to create; beings who usually succeed in new endeavors only after taking risks and failing; and beings for whom even the Bible cannot provide certainty because, among other factors, it contains ruses. The Bible may be inerrant, but its readers are not.

The eighteenth-century hasidic master, the Maggid of Mezeritch, put it this way: "God, in His infinite love, restrains His power to enlighten, so that man may receive step by step, stage by stage, the revelation of what lies beyond his limits: that is the way of a father teaching his son to walk."[28] Our religious understanding is fallible at every stage, so we should strive to discern a progressive divine revelation. We should not rest only on past understanding.

Julius Guttmann observed that "by ascribing to Biblical laws the purpose of combating heathen ideas and practices, and by referring for this to sources which for him were documents of ancient paganism, [Maimonides] was the first to attempt an explanation of at any rate part of Biblical legislation by means of the comparative study of religion." Guttmann further noted that John Spencer then developed this approach in the seventeenth century "under constant reference to the authority of Maimonides, and through his agency it gained decisive influence on the comparative study of Biblical religion in modern times."[29]

Maimonides's philosophy for a perplexed savant was a guide to the heavens; but in the *Mishneh Torah*, his Code of Law, he was a father to the people, still teaching them how to walk on earth. He continued there the Torah's "gracious ruse," presenting the idea of animal sacrifice in the Temple of Holiness as still valid. He judged his contemporaries rightly; they were not ready to abandon the idea.

Indeed, the right-wing Orthodox still affirm the idea of animal sacrifice, and some in Israel are preparing to resume the practice. But the idea is offensive to the non-Orthodox, the large majority of today's Jews. Characteristically, the Modern Orthodox still say the prayer for the reinstitution of animal sacrifice but are otherwise silent on the matter. The Conservatives also characteristically hedge on the issue; they pray for the restoration of the Temple of Holiness and mention the sacrifices, but they put the sacrifices in the past tense.

Rabbi Louis Jacobs writes to me as follows:

Ben Zion Bokser referred me many years ago to an astonishing comment of Rav Kook [1865–

1935] in his *Siddur* [prayer book] (after the section on *korbanot* [sacrifices]) where Kook says
that there will be no animal sacrifices in the
Messianic age, only *menahot* [meal offerings].
And yet in the same *Siddur* Kook includes
prayers for the restoration of animal sacrifices.
All very puzzling.

Jacobs is suggesting that Maimonides had inspired Kook's view of animal sacrifice, and I think
that Maimonides had also inspired Kook's views of
the elite and the principle of development. For, as
Jacobs writes elsewhere: "Virtually alone among
Orthodox Rabbis, Kook warmly espoused the theory
of evolution, believing this to be in accord with the
Kabbalistic doctrine that all worlds are moving gradually from the lower to the higher." He quotes Kook:
"it is not at all strange [for the elite] to understand
by analogy that . . . the physical universe proceeds by
the same method of development as the spiritual"
because the elite have "always tended to see things in
terms of development."

Abraham Isaac Kook, vegetarian, kabbalist, and
first Ashkenazi Chief Rabbi of Palestine (appointed in
1921), was a controversial figure. Jacobs notes that
the "Rabbis of the old school, to which, in a sense,
Kook belonged, were opposed to his encouragement
of the secular Zionists and to his attempt at bridging
the gap between the Jewish tradition and the world of
science and technology."[30] Such opposition still exists.

Maimonides in turn was inspired by Rav, who
had held that halakhah needed to respond creatively
to serious cultural changes. Rav had also influenced
Maimonides to view all the Laws teleologically, but
to see that a purpose for the particulars of some Laws

could never be found. Thus, Rav had said (Genesis Rabbah 44:1): "The *mitzvot* [God's commandments] were given only as a means of refining men. For what difference does it make to God whether one slaughters an animal [ritually] from the front or from the back of the neck?"

Maimonides rendered the goal of "refining men" as follows: "The Law as a whole aims at two things: the welfare of the soul ['acquiring correct opinions'] and the welfare of the body [improving 'ways of living one with another']." Although sacrifices had long ago served the welfare of the soul, he said, "no cause will ever be found for the fact that one particular sacrifice consists in a *lamb* and another in a *ram* and that the number of victims should be one particular number." Maimonides added the following text with an unstated but unmistakable reference to Rav: "What does it matter to [God] that animals are slaughtered by cutting their neck in front or in the back?"[31]

Medieval Maimonides and the ancient tradition he deepened thus held the modern metaphysical basis of history—the new may exhibit improvement or even originality. Divine revelation is progressive. God and humans periodically create Law to adjust to significant cultural changes, and, as a true partner, God sometimes yields to the human partners.

The Talmud emphasizes the last point in the following story. Rabbi Eliezer b. Hyrcanus, our epitome of halakhic conservatism, once brought forth many arguments to support his halakhic decision, but the rabbis were not persuaded. So he said, "Let this carob tree prove that the halakhah agrees with me," and the tree was torn 100 cubits out of its place— some say 400 cubits. The rabbis replied: "Proof cannot be brought from a carob tree." Then he said, "Let this stream of water prove that the halakhah agrees with me," and the stream flowed backward. The rabbis replied: "Proof cannot be brought from a stream of water."

Rabbi Eliezer persisted: "Let these schoolhouse walls prove that the halakhah agrees with me," and the walls inclined to fall. But Rabbi Joshua rebuked the walls: "Why do you interfere in a scholarly dispute?! Hence, in honor of Rabbi Joshua the walls did not fall, but in honor of Rabbi Eliezer they did not become upright; and they still stand inclined.

Finally, Rabbi Eliezer said, "Let Heaven prove that the halakhah agrees with me." Whereupon a Voice from Heaven declared: "Why do you dispute with Rabbi Eliezer, for the halakhah always agrees with him!" Rabbi Joshua stood up and said: "*It is not in heaven*" (Deut. 30:12). What did he mean? Said Rabbi Jeremiah: "We disregard a Voice from Heaven, for You have already given the Torah at Mt. Sinai; and in it You wrote—'*After the majority must one incline*'" (Exodus 23:2).

Some time later, Rabbi Nathan met Elijah and asked him: "What did the Holy One, blessed be He, do in that hour?" Elijah replied: "He laughed and said, 'My children have defeated Me, My children have defeated Me'" (Bava Metzia 59b).[32]

This text is extreme in implying that God no longer shares in the creation of Law. As Rackman says, other "texts as well as experience support the view that, while there shall never be another Torah, sages relied on Divine help and even apocalyptic prophecy to discover God's will in countless Halachik situations."[33] There is thus a genuine partnership between God and humans.

You may wonder what important matter was in dispute between the rabbis and Rabbi Eliezer. Well, they differed on whether Aknai's oven was ritually clean. Children of the Enlightenment will greet this information with sarcasm, whereas those who take religious ritual seriously will want to understand why the epiphany occurred here and not in any other halakhic dispute.

The explanation emerges at the story's end. On the very day after the dispute, the rabbis burned in fire as unclean all the objects which Rabbi Eliezer had declared ritually clean. (Come now, why did you Children of the Enlightenment think that Rabbi Eliezer was the one who had declared Aknai's oven unclean?) Then the rabbis voted and excommunicated Rabbi Eliezer.

Disaster occurred on that day. Things burned up wherever Rabbi Eliezer cast his eyes. Rabbi Gamaliel, the head of the Jewish community and Rabbi Eliezer's brother-in-law, was aboard a ship when a huge wave came up and was about to drown him. He felt that this was happening because he had been the prime mover of the excommunication, and so he exclaimed: "Master of the Universe: You know full well that I have acted neither for my honor nor for my family's honor—but for Your honor, so that dissension may not multiply in Israel!" The raging sea subsided (Bava Metzia 59b).

Neither the subject of the dispute nor the dispute per se led to the epiphany and excommunication. The rabbis honored halakhic argument on every subject. But life demands that such debate end in law, in a decision that obligates all in practice, including those who had opposed it—which makes them the loyal opposition; and the law was determined regularly by the majority view of the rabbis. Rabbi Eliezer, however, refused in this case to yield to the majority.

The epiphany and excommunication occurred here and not elsewhere because Rabbi Eliezer's opposition was disloyal here; only here was his opposition perceived as a threat to the rule of law and to social harmony.[34] The rabbis held that these values superseded Rabbi Eliezer's ritual truth, and God finally agreed; hence, social harmony and the rule of law were for the rabbis religiously humanistic values. The ancient modern tradition of religious humanism entails a strong belief in the dignity of people as autonomous and as God's partners, and a trust in the people's will and power to "repair the world."

The Talmud advocates religious humanism also in other situations. For example, the rabbis ruled that one should always praise the bride as beautiful and graceful, even if it violates the biblical prohibition against lying because "one should always be pleasant with people" (Ketubot 16b–17a). One should always be a *mentsh*, the Yiddish word for such humanism.

Here is another talmudic example of *mentshlikhkeit* superseding truthfulness. Rav Judah said in the name of Samuel: "The learned do not tell the truth in the following three matters—a tractate, sexuality, and hospitality" (Bava Metzia 23b–24a). Tosafot, a medieval commentary, explains: a scholar may falsely concede ignorance when his knowledge is contested; a scholar may falsely attribute his absence from the academy, say to illness, instead of truthfully to sexuality; and a scholar may falsely report a visit as inhospitable in order to deter the unworthy from draining a very generous host. *Mentshlikhkeit* thus includes also modesty, propriety, and "peaceful ways."

My final example concerns the three-year argument between the School of Hillel and the School of Shammai, in which each claimed that its rulings determined the halakhah. "Then a Voice from Heaven proclaimed: 'The words of both are the living words of God, but the law follows the ruling of the School of Hillel.'" Why? The Talmud explains: "because they were gentle, modest, studied the opinions of both schools, and mentioned the words of the School of Shammai before their own" (Erubin 13b). *Mentshlikhkeit* is here, too, the deciding factor in law.

This story is striking on three points. First, it conflicts with our previous story, wherein the rabbis ruled the Voice from Heaven out of order in their halakhic disputes. This story is one of those other texts to which Rackman alluded, wherein the "sages relied on Divine help" in determining halakhah. But how can the rabbis know, much less be certain, when to rely on a Voice from Heaven and when not to rely on it?

Second, the criterion for deciding halakhah in the previous examples was the humanistic character of the law, whereas the criterion here is the humanistic character of the law's proponents. But should not the proponents' character be irrelevant in creating law? A humanistic character may give promise of a humanistic law, but the promise is not certain to be fulfilled. For humanistic characters, being human, are not always in character. Furthermore, even when in character, they often disagree among themselves about the law.

Still, the Talmud's humanism is a religious one, in which the proponent's righteous character is fittingly required for creating law. Hence, *mentshlikhkeit* became the decisive factor here because the halakhic views of both schools were acceptable.

And that is the third striking point in our text—
that conflicting versions of the law are both "the
living words of God." For instance, either school's
ruling on the minimum size of a *sukkah* was acceptable to God, but expediency required a uniform practice. This indicates that both schools were inspired by
God's purpose and that God cares more about the
ritual's purpose than about its details, which agrees
with Rav's and Maimonides's outlook.

Either school's ruling on the *sukkah*'s size would
accomplish God's purpose; whether that is to remind
us of God's protection of the Israelites in the wilder-
ness or to remind the rich of the poor. But here most
authorities accept the School of Shammai's ruling
(Maimonides, *Mishneh Torah*, "Laws of Shofar, Sukkah
and Lulav," 6:8; also Y. T. Vidal, *Maggid Mishneh*).
Ah, these rabbis, even when they accept the Voice
from Heaven's ruling, they do not accept it in all
cases. There is uncertainty about God's purpose, and
there is uncertainty about the range of His Voice.

This approach to ritual is the antithesis of theurgy;
it seeks God's purpose rather than the control of
supernatural forces through esoteric formulae. We can
intend our practice of rituals and other precepts to
fulfill God's purpose even in cases where the purpose
is unknown. This talmudic story was most likely
another source for Maimonides's rationale of the
Torah's rituals.

This approach to ritual is the antithesis of obsessional neurosis, too, which is "characterized by
compulsive ideas or irresistible urges and often manifested in the ritualistic performance of certain acts."
This way of religious ritual is in the region of love,
whereas the obsessional way of ritual is in the region
of guilt and fear. Those who are obsessively religious

focus anxiously on the ritual's mechanics rather than its purpose. They are so deeply immersed in the body of ritual that they cannot see its glimmer.

Maimonides knew that very few of his contemporaries were ready for his approach to the Torah's rituals, so he wrote *The Guide* cryptically. For instance, he expected that most would have dispensed with their faith had they understood him to believe that "God can dispense with them [i.e., rituals of animal sacrifice]."[35] Many today are still not ready to "dispense with them." The experience of East European Jews who immigrated to the United States between 1880 and 1920, most still at the lower stages of religious development, supports Maimonides's expectation.

Nathan Glazer observes that the popular form of Judaism which had been taught to these immigrants consisted mainly of "a rigid set of rituals to cover one's entire life" and that it had tended to "obscure the meaning [purpose] of ritual." Hence, when so many of them, who were the Orthodox parents and grandparents of the great majority of U.S. Jews, found that forsaking the rituals—working on the Sabbath, shaving, and abandoning traditional dress—was more convenient in the United States, their old faith and "entire [Jewish] way of life disintegrated"; it seems that to them nothing was "more important [in religion] than the rituals established by God's word."[36]

That is how one extreme approach to ritual jeopardizes traditional Judaism. The opposite extreme, the exclusively teleological approach, which is an interested approach, also jeopardizes traditional Judaism because it disregards the ritual's intraested values, whether mystical or esthetic or emotional or ethnic. This extreme path could lead to divergent goals and observances, or even to an inordinate individualism, which might sunder the traditional community.

In Orthodoxy, Glazer notes, "the holy *community*" touches and moves people "and brings them back to the faith," and keeping the Law is that community's hallmark. This is a "central" and "somewhat distinctive" religious pattern, different from Protestantism, for instance, where the return to faith means "the acceptance of beliefs."[37] Hence, significant divergence of religious practice would jeopardize the cohesion of the Orthodox community.

The extreme teleological approach misses the heart of religious experience—emotion, holiness, and wholeness. A traditional ritual is not merely a means; it has emotional value in its own right. On reciting in the *sukkah* the special welcome to the seven "guests of the festival"—Abraham, Isaac, Jacob, Joseph, Moses, Aaron, and David—one's deceased parents also appear in memory; and the parents and their children smile at each other. And on drinking the *kiddush* wine from father's silver cup, father and offspring kiss.

A traditional ritual can have the value also of holiness in its own right, provided that it does not violate a later, more mature sensibility—as the return to animal sacrifice would do. A ritual can be hallowed for traditional Jews even if it no longer serves the original purpose because it was once chosen by God and "established by His holy word." It retains an aura of holiness, as the wedding ring retains an aura of love after the beloved's death.

The halakhah can thus be humanistic and conservative: it can conserve the long and solid trunk of Judaism's identity even for modern humanistic platforms because the rabbis' halakhic authority is wide, deep, and flexible.

In conclusion, I have argued that we cannot attain certainty in religion, in any of its forms. Indeed, Alan T. Davies, Protestant theologian, avers: "All profound theistic (and biblical) faith embraces doubt as one of its elements. According to the New Testament, the death of Jesus was the death of a troubled theist who felt himself forsaken by God."[38] I have also argued that traditional Jewish sources support Modern Orthodoxy as much as they do right-wing Orthodoxy, and, indeed, that they could support an even more modern and humanistic Orthodoxy.

Rabbi Rackman, the solitary herald of such an Orthodoxy, also avers: "A Jew dare not live with absolute certainty [i.e., absolute certitude], not only because certainty is the hallmark of the fanatic and Judaism abhors fanaticism, but also because doubt is good for the human soul, its humility, and consequently its greater potential ultimately to discover its Creator."[39]

Even Rabbi Moses Feinstein, right-wing Orthodoxy's foremost halakhic decisor of the past generation, had subtly begun to move toward modern Orthodoxy. Norma Baumel Joseph notes in a study of his Responsa that he warns decisors to "acknowledge that there is no guarantee of absolute . . . validity to [their] rulings," for other or later decisors may with equal validity give a different ruling. Indeed, "given his initial hesitation, [Feinstein] makes a startling conclusion": he is "obligated to use his knowledge and education to decide . . . practical law . . . according to his ability and insight." Joseph concludes: "within [his] framework of a denial of change and affirmation of the immutability of law, alteration and modification is taking place."[40]

Some courageous, moderate, religious liberals and conservatives, as well as secularists, confront our essential uncertainties and accept into their life meanings the idea that "doubt is good for the human soul"; and they tend to respect spiritual beliefs that diverge from their own. But what is the likelihood of most people tolerating each other's spiritual beliefs?

Karen Armstrong's *The Battle for God* gives an historical, sociological, political, and theological account of the conflicts between the forces of modernity, religious as well as secular, and fundamentalism. Both sides have been hostile and at times oppressive toward each other, but, as one might suspect, modernity has been dominant in Modernity. Even fundamentalists have incorporated "modern, innovative, and modernizing" ways into religion, but their doctrines and practices have been "rooted in [the] fear" that "the secularists were about to wipe them out." The modern world "seems Godless, drained of meaning, and even satanic to a fundamentalist."[41]

I think, however, that the deepest fear underlying the hostility toward another's spiritual orientation is the fear of facing the uncertainty of the truth or value of one's own life meaning. This applies as much to liberals, secularists, and atheists as to fundamentalists; all must face this deepest uncertainty alike if we are largely to reduce spiritual enmity. Armstrong also aims at the reduction of such enmity. She concludes her erudite and insightful book with its leitmotif:

> If fundamentalists must evolve a more compassionate assessment of their enemies in order to be true to their religious traditions, secularists must also be more faithful to the benevolence, tolerance, and respect for humanity which characterizes modern culture at its best, and address themselves more empathetically to the fears,

anxieties, and needs which so many of their fundamentalist neighbors experience but which no society can safely ignore.[42]

Although Armstrong's history of the conflict is unbiased, her solution is patronizing. Yes, she urges both parties to show more compassion, but she always calls only the liberals to address the fears of the other party, apparently believing that only her party is sufficiently adult to do that. Her belief is unwarranted; fundamentalists are as much, or as little, capable as the liberals in this matter, too. Liberals, as much as fundamentalists, are in need of cognitive modesty.

Finally, the other party's fear is not the most important to address in order to reduce religious hostility; it is rather the facing of one's own fear of life meaning's uncertainty that is most important—and most difficult.

Chapter 5

Wholeness: Primordial and Vicarial

Humans were much like Rainer Maria Rilke's animal before they developed a sense of individuality:

> If the animal
> > coming toward us so surely
> > > from another direction
>
> had our kind of consciousness
> > he'd drag us around in his sway.
> > > But his being
>
> is infinite to him
> > incomprehensible, and without
> > > a sense of his condition
>
> pure as his gaze.
> > And where we see the future
> > > he sees everything

and himself *in* everything
healed and whole
forever.

The "kind of consciousness" humans had before
the Axial Age also was "without a sense of [their]
condition"—of their lack of individuality. The question of life's meaning did not arise because they had
an organic relation to the universe. They did not
require redemption because they saw "everything and
[themselves] *in* everything healed and whole forever."
They did not "see the future" as uncertain, insecure,
because their world view was mythic.

And yet within the animal "a huge sadness" exists
because a tender memory of life in the womb clings to
him. Preindividualistic humans, too, had an inchoate
recollection that whatever they were striving for "was
once closer and truer," was once "breath" and not "dis-
tance." We, who are daily reminded of our individuality,
of our separateness, sense more sharply that "After the
first home / the second seems hybrid / and windy."

We are "spectators, always everywhere," and Rilke
asks, "What has turned us around this way?"

We never have
even for one single day
that pure space before us
that flowers can open

endlessly into.
It's always *world*
it's never a nowhere

where there isn't
any "no," any "don't"
never the pure.[1]

Accordingly, I note, only Adam and Eve could have had a paradisal life because they alone did not suffer separation from the womb, which cannot be said even of Jesus. And their spiritual exile from Eden began with the sound of the first "don't." Moral rules have no place in Paradise, but they are essential in our world.

So, Rilke asks, why is it that, given the chance, we would choose human existence over any other kind— even that of a gnat or a flower? "Oh, not because happiness is real," since it is only the forerunner of ruin; but because "everything here / all that's disappearing / seems to need us / to concern us / in some strange way / we, who disappear / even faster."

>   It's one time
>   for each thing
>   and *only* one.
>   Once and no more.
>
>   And the same for us:
>   *once.*
>   Then never again.
>
>   But this once having been
>   even though only once
>   having been on earth
>
>   seems as though
>   it can't be undone.

We are more intimate with nature and things than an angel can be because we share transitoriness with them. An angel, however, is more intimate with the unsayable than we can be. Hence, we should praise the world to the angel and speak the words "with an intensity / the things themselves / never dreamed they'd express"; "*Here* is the time / for the *sayable* / here is its home." Here is the poet's abode, not the angel's.

> Show him, then,
>   some simple thing
>   shaped by its passage
>
> through generations
>   that lives as a belonging
>   near the hand, in the gaze.
>
> Tell him of Things.
>   He'll stand more astonished
>   than you did
>
> beside the rope-maker
>   in Rome, or the potter
>   by the Nile.[2]

Life's meaning inheres in the wind, not in eternity. "Our task," Rilke writes to his Polish translator, "is so deeply and so passionately to impress upon ourselves this provisional and perishable earth, that its essential being will arise again 'invisibly' in us."[3]

> And these things
>   that take their life
>
> from impermanence
>   they understand
>   that you're praising them:

perishing, they trust
       to us—the most
              perishable of all—

for their preservation.
       They want us to change them
          completely

inside our invisible hearts
       into—oh endlessly—
          into ourselves!

Whoever we might
       turn out to be
          at the end.

Earth, isn't this
       what you want:
          rising up

inside us invisibly
       once more?[4]

Rilke was a restless traveler and essentially solitary. Stefan Zweig writes: "It was difficult to reach Rilke. He had no house, no address where one could find him, no home, no steady lodging, no office. He was always on his way through the world, and no one, not even himself, knew in advance which direction it would take."[5] But then he learned what his direction was to be and followed it.

Once, he had been unable to perform his task completely, but that changed: "Earth, my love / I will do it. / Believe me / your springtimes / are no longer needed / to win me—*one* / just one, is already / too much for my blood. / I have been yours / unable to say so / for a long time now. / You were right / always / and affable Death / is your own / holy notion." Now, Rilke says, he lives neither on his past nor on his future, but "Being / in excess / wells up / in my heart."[6] Now he is able to perform his task, to keep his promise of transforming nature into himself, into his poetry.

Now, Death is "affable," easy to approach; it is Life's mate. If one has loved existence, prized its transitoriness, and embraced it fully in consciousness, then one can find sorrow and death amiable. Rilke trusts that he will not lament at his end:

> Oh you nights
> that I grieved through
> how much you will
> mean to me then.

> Disconsolate sisters
> why didn't I kneel
> more fully

> to accept you
> and lose myself more
> in your loosened hair?

> How we squander our sorrows
> gazing beyond them
> into the sad

> wastes of duration
> to see if maybe
> they have a limit.

But they are
> our winter foliage
>> our dark evergreens

one of the seasons
> of our secret year
>> —and not only a season

they are situation,
> settlement, lair,
>> soil, home.[7]

He writes to his Polish translator: "Death is the *side of life* that is turned away from us: we must try to achieve the fullest consciousness of our existence, which is at home in the *two unseparated realms, inexhaustibly nourished by both.* . . ."[8] Still, in the final Elegy's imaginative journey through Death, he calls that realm "Pain City."[9]

Rilke heeded the development of Freudian psychology, but he viewed the psychology of birth differently from the early psychoanalysts. They saw birth as the prototype of traumatic separation; but he saw it as also an enduring sadness, a clinging, wistful sense of lost wholeness, of a vanished union that was "incredibly tender." Our biological need for a meaning of life springs from this experience of lost wholeness, but the longing for such meaning, for wholeness, emerged together with the individualism of the Axial Age.

The wistful sense of lost wholeness comprises one's awareness of individuality, of separation, and one's longing for a return to wholeness. This sense is plain in a great work of the Axial Age, in the *Symposium*'s myth of love. Aristophanes, a character in Plato's dialogue, speaks:

The sexes were originally three, men, women, and the union of the two; . . . . Terrible was [the latter's] strength and swiftness; and they were essaying to scale heaven and attack the gods. Doubt reigned in the celestial councils; the gods were divided between the desire of quelling the pride of man and the fear of losing the sacrifices. At last Zeus hit upon an expedient. Let us cut them in two, he said, then they will only have half their strength, and we shall have twice as many sacrifices. . . . The two halves went about looking for one another, and were ready to die of hunger in one another's arms. . . . Those who come from the man-woman are lascivious and adulterous; those who come from the woman form female attachments; those who are a section of the male follow the male and embrace him, and in him all their desires center. . . . But if Hephaestus were to come to them with his instruments and propose that they should be melted into one and remain one here and hereafter, they would acknowledge that this was the very expression of their want. *For love is the desire of the whole, and the pursuit of the whole is called love.*[10]

Romantic love, like all life meanings, is an intraested involvement that returns us vicariously to primordial wholeness, taking the sonata form of A B A; but it cannot attain the complete and relatively simple accord that marked life in the womb. Still, its accord encircles a large dimension of existence, thus making it a *life* meaning, whereas those instances of the sonata form that encompass little dimensions of our existence are not life meanings because they provide only a narrow wholeness, a small completion.

Romantic love is a life meaning while it lasts or is pursued.

"You can't go home, again"—that is, not in every way. We can return vicariously to original wholeness, but we come back complex and conscious. The musical notes in the sonata form's first and final A sections are seldom entirely the same, but we perceive them differently even when they are identical— as in J.S. Bach's "Goldberg Variations." As T. S. Eliot said: "We shall not cease from exploration / And the end of all our exploring / Will be to arrive where we started / And know the place for the first time."[11]

Some, however, prefer an original wholeness over a later wholeness. For example, Catholic doctrine holds that, before entering Heaven, sinners who have repented and been forgiven must pass through Purgatory, a place or state after death wherein the sins are expiated by suffering, whereas those who have been wholly sinless enter Heaven directly. A talmudic sage, Rabbi Yohanan, also believed that the wholly righteous are more worthy than the penitent. These beliefs favor original innocence over restored innocence, and thus cohere with the premodern view of the metaphysical basis of history.

Other talmudic sages, however, favored restored innocence over original innocence, which coheres with the modern view of the metaphysical basis of history. Thus, Rabbi Abbahu said: "In the place where penitents stand even the wholly righteous cannot stand" (Berakkoth, 34b). Moreover:

> Rabbi Abbahu said: "The Holy One, blessed be He, kept creating worlds and destroying them, until He created these [heaven and earth]. Then God said: "These please Me; those did not."

> Rabbi Pinhas attributed Rabbi Abbahu's view
> to the statement: "And God saw everything that
> He had made, and, behold, it was very good"
> [Genesis, I,31]—these please Me; those did not.
> (Gen. R. 9:2)

So, we should not be surprised that Rabbi Abbahu
valued penitents more than the sinless because he
believed that even God learns from mistakes.

Also, Rabbi Meir said: "Great is a person's repentance, for it brings forgiveness to all the world's
sins" (Yoma, 86b). One gathers that these, the penitents, bring forgiveness to the world's sins, but those,
the wholly sinless, do not; perhaps because the latter
are of another species, never having experienced sin
and forgiveness. These rabbis favored restored innocence over original innocence, as do I.

The Baal Shem Tov, founder of modern Hasidism,
spoke similarly more than a millennium later to a
zaddik who preached admonishing sermons: "What
do you know about admonishing! You yourself have
remained unacquainted with sin all the days of your
life, and you have had nothing to do with the people
around you—how should you know what sin is!"[12]
Friedrich Nietzsche put it this way: "One is most
dishonest to one's god: he is not *allowed* to sin."[13]

Sins and mistakes are primary vehicles of growth
in morality and cognition. They are B sections in
moral and cognitive sonata forms: they carry us from
simplicity to complexity, from naivety to sophistica-
tion; and the tensions they generate—a longing for
the old, familiar innocence together with a drive to
explore the new—can, with effort, find release and
integration in the final, changed, A' section.

This process is similar to that of the sonata form in music, whose Muse, via Adolph B. Marx, first named the form. Felix Salzer writes:

> Hence, the development section [B] is ultimately a section of transitional motion. This fact makes it necessary for the motion . . . to demonstrate an unusual degree of direction in its drive towards the recapitulation [A']. On the other hand, the structural demand to prolong one single chord or one short progression for the purpose of achieving an adequate formal section, engenders an element of expanse and retard. The artistic struggle between these two contrasting factors of dramatic drive and expansion creates the tension so characteristic for the development sections of pieces in sonata form, and which furthermore explains why the entry of the recapitulation in a good sonata movement has an effect of release following accumulated tension.[14]

Murray Perahia informs me of Charles Rosen's broader view of tension in the sonata form. Rosen sees the exposition, development, and recapitulation sections functioning, respectively, "as *opposition, intensification,* and *resolution*": a clear opposition between themes is intensified and then resolved.[15] Perahia comments keenly: "This implies that the 'sins and mistakes that are primary vehicles of growth in morality and cognition' are implicit already in the first section with its opposition of first and second themes." Such is the case with so many of our undertakings, but resolution occurs there much less frequently; and in this lies a major appeal of the sonata. Still, the term "sonata form" applies loosely also to cases where opposition and tension are absent in the first section—for example, to what Rosen calls "the basic ternary ABA form."[16]

The sonata form is a basic structure of human life. It is identity in transition, continuity in shift. It is conservative change[17]: modifying, because it values the present and the future, but only modifying, because it values the past. As William James said of one whose stock of beliefs is opposed by a new experience: "He saves as much of [the stock] as he can, for in this matter of belief we are all extreme conservatives." One searches for a new idea that mediates between the stock and the new experience "with a minimum of disturbance" to the former. Even "the most violent revolutions in an individual's beliefs leave most of his old order standing."[18]

But what is it about primordial wholeness that impels us to seek it again vicariously through life meanings? It is our archetypal experience of being wholly integrated with our whole world—"for womb / is everything." Then birth shatters that small world, and the infant inchoately senses a lost security and contentment. We are thrust into an immense world of dangers and challenges, where the self's expanding powers will never be wholly adequate to one's world.

Still becoming fearful of their individuality and separation, nearly three millennia into the Axial Age, many acquire union and life meaning automatically or unquestioningly from the established culture. Only a relatively few confront the problem of life's meaning deliberately, independently, and courageously. But no one regains the completeness of *primordial wholeness*, for no one's powers can ever again be *wholly integrated* with, *wholly adequate* to, one's *whole world*. I wish to suggest by the preceding italicized words why many describe a person's ideal state as one of "wholeness," since the word's meaning is seldom explained.

This account of our passage through birth is refracted in myth. Socrates, a character in Plato's *Meno*, cites priests and poets in support of his doctrine that learning is only recollection. "The truth of all things always existed in the soul," he claims, but we forget them all at birth; afterwards, we *recall* some and mistakenly call that "learning."[19] We regain only some of the knowledge that was whole before birth, but such recollection, Socrates says, is our great virtue.

Such myths reflect the person's journey to birth, whereas other myths reflect society's journey to the Axial Age. The social problems caused by the origin of individualism led the Axial Age to Golden Age myths, which wistfully picture a primeval, innocent, organic, and wholly happy society; but the idea of a Golden Age arises also from the individual's experience of primordial wholeness.

Utopian myths emerge from the same social and individual contexts, but they focus on the future. They are schemes for attaining a perfect society, inspired by the yearning for a perfect return to primordial wholeness. No wonder that these schemes must fail, or worse. That is the point of Plato's Golden Age and utopian myths.

Thus, the Stranger in Plato's *Statesman* narrates the Myth of Kronos. He describes a distant past (pre-Axial) Age when the god Kronos reigned and rigidly controlled everything. As in the (pre-Axial) Garden of Eden, all things came "without man's labor," and fruits were had "without stint from trees and bushes which needed no cultivation. . . ." "Men rose up anew into life out of the earth" and for the most part

required no clothing. There were "no political con-
stitutions and no personal possession of wives and
children." And, as with Isaiah's Messianic vision (of
the post-Axial Age), "savagery was nowhere to be
found nor preying of creature on creature, nor did
war rage nor any strife whatsoever." It was a Golden
Age of primeval wholeness.

Then the wholly regulated rule of Kronos was
overthrown, and the reign of Zeus (the Axial Age)
began—with its toils, tribulations, and hazards. And
in that reign, which still prevails, "the universe must
take sole responsibility and control of its course,"
and "its constituent elements [must] achieve by their
own power, so far as they might, conception, procre-
ation, and rearing of young."

The Stranger wonders, "which of these two
[reigns] makes for greater happiness?" He thinks that
"the crucial question is—did the nurslings of Kronos
make a right use of their time?" Their happiness would
have been "a thousandfold greater than ours" had
they spent their abundant leisure searching for truth
and wisdom. But if, after taking their fill of eating
and drinking, their discussions had been "of the kind
that the surviving stories make them out to have
been, then . . . it is equally clear what our verdict must
be"[20]—namely, that *our* lot would be the happier.

Plato also strongly implies that there would be in
paradise no stimulus to pursue truth and wisdom. Indeed, as I have argued elsewhere,[21] Plato shows in the
Republic, especially in its Myth of Er, that any utopia,
any rigidly regulated society, even one ruled by lovers of
wisdom, would be calamitous for us in the Axial Age.
The myth concludes the dialogue and is its epitome.

Er relates that souls in the afterworld were select-
ing their next life, and the first chose with little thought

a horrible life. On perceiving that "he was fated, among other evils, to devour his own children," he beat his breast and blamed his misfortune on "chance and the gods, and everything rather than himself." Now, "he was one of those who came from heaven, and in a former life had dwelt in a *well-ordered State*, virtuous from habit only, and without philosophy." Much the same happened to the majority of those who came from heaven, for "they had never been schooled by trial." But those "who came from earth, having themselves suffered and seen others suffer, were not in a hurry to choose"—and chose much better.[22]

Plato thus shows that our best course to happiness in the Axial Age is a wise self-determination and not a benign dependence. And this not despite the entailed hazards, sufferings, and tribulations, but because of them; they are essential to understanding, appreciating, and dealing wisely with our world—and essential for our emotional growth.

Rilke must have imbibed Plato's myths: the Golden Age was in the womb, Utopia is no place, and our place is "hybrid and windy." This unanticipated return to Plato's antiutopianism moves me yet again. A half century has passed since John H. Randall, Jr.'s lecture on Plato's antiutopianism in the *Republic* first moved me. My response, intellectual and emotional, was so intense that it could not be wholly explained by the novelty and cogency of Randall's interpretation. Only forty years later did I better understand my response[23]: Randall's Plato had occasioned a confrontation with my perfectionism.

Now, I realize that Plato was for me more than an antidote to neurotic control; it was also an inchoate release of a life meaning. I would try to pursue a life of wise self-determination: one that would accept my limits in directing the future and would be balanced by greater intraestedness—for instance, by Plato's conviction that "virtue is its own reward." I have attained self-determination, although not much wisdom, but the pursuit itself, the journey, has turned out to be a life meaning.

Now, I realize also that Plato's myths embody main points of my thesis: a belief in a prenatal state of wholeness and in a postnatal striving to regain wholeness. But though postnatal and Axial Age wholeness entails risk and complexity, we would not wish to return to the womb or become "a gnat or a flower."

Many of us have more than one meaning of life; otherwise, Durkheim would have had to analyze masses of mass suicides and not just rises in suicide rates. It is the other meanings of life that sustain us during anomy, such as creativity or "generational responsibility"—Paul Tsongas's mission "to ensure that life passes on, enhanced, cherished, protected."[24] I suggest that Durkheim's suicides had one overwhelming meaning of life—that which had been deregulated or disintegrated. This would at least partially explain what he left unexplained: What caused those particular people but not others to commit anomic or egoistic suicide?

Most of us cannot understand the minds of terrorists who murder harmless and innocent people. I suggest that they do so in part because of an overwhelming meaning of life. Robert Conquest's *Reflections on a Ravaged Century* exposes such a mind in an apologist for terrorism. Josef Joffe writes in a review of the book:

> The book's most poignant passages quote from
> a recent interview with the Marxist historian Eric

Hobsbawn. Had he known back in 1934 that "millions of people are dying in the Soviet experiment," would he have renounced Communism? "Probably not," replied Hobsbawn. And why not? Because "the chance of a new world being born in great suffering would still have been worth backing." So it would have been worth the sacrifice of 15 million, 20 million? "Yes."[25]

Would you trust him with truth?

Such an overwhelming meaning of life is shared by some who kill themselves—by those who commit anomic or egoistic suicide. This account coheres with that which sees suicide as rage against others internalized. But we must not overlook the role of the soul's evil force in terrorism. My revulsion with terrorism is a force behind this book.

A life meaning is neither necessarily for life nor necessarily desirable for life. Passage through the stages of life may leave a life meaning behind or form a new one, and such creativity may happen also during a single stage. Indeed, creativity itself tends to be a life meaning for creators. How awesome: birth, becoming fully created, shattered our primordial wholeness, but creating, giving birth to beauty, for example, can bring us vicarious wholeness.

I have focused on life meanings as they issue from the person because there is no way to verify claims of a universal meaning of life, of an objective purpose that issues from God or the cosmos. Even those who agree that there is such a purpose disagree on what the purpose is. Others believe, I among them, that the cosmos just is and that God's existence is not evident, that the cosmos is silent about purpose.[26] But all such claims or beliefs and their contraries are uncertain and a matter of faith, and one chooses a faith even if one is unaware of choosing.

Many repress the intrinsic uncertainty of their faith as well as the fallible, nonrational basis of their choice, thereby diminishing their possibilities of self-realization; for the consciousness of uncertainty and free choice are aspects of the human consciousness of individuality. Hence, I consider the Axial Age as not yet having reached maturity, let alone as having been transcended.

Karen Armstrong thinks otherwise. She notes, for example, the widespread change of worldview that occurred directly after World War I. For then "no thinking person could [any longer] be serenely optimistic about the progress of civilization" since "the people of the West [had] looked straight into the void that some had sensed for decades"; and yet this was also a time of "unparalleled creativity and astonishing achievements in the arts and sciences, revealing the full flowering of the modern spirit."

Religion, too, was deeply affected. Armstrong observes that "the most prescient realized [the impossibility] for fully modernized people to be religious in the old way," and that "if they wanted to be religious, they would have to develop rites, beliefs, and practices that spoke to them in their radically altered circumstances." "Just as people in the first Axial Age (c. 700–200 B.C.E.) had found that the old paganism no longer worked in the new conditions of their period and had evolved the great confessional faiths, so too, in this second Axial Age [which began in the Age of Enlightenment], there was a similar challenge."[27]

True, modernity's developments of consciousness were very important, but I do not consider them sufficiently profound to be called a new Axial Age; they were not as radical as the emergence of the

consciousness of individuality. I would designate neither modernity nor postmodernity as a new Axial
Age; I see them, rather, as a "flowering" of the consciousness of individuality that arose nearly three
millennia ago.

Ewert Cousins believes, however, that we are now
entering a Second Axial Age. He writes that on "the
eve of the twenty-first century, we can discern another transformation of consciousness [which] is so
profound and far-reaching that I call it the Second
Axial Period." Individual consciousness emerged and
developed in the First Axial Age, and "now it is global consciousness" that is emerging.

Following Teilhard de Chardin, Cousins sees "that
a shift in the forces of evolution [has] occurred over
the past [two] hundred years"—from divergence to
convergence. Humans have diverged for millennia,
creating separate nations and cultures, but now we
have "no other course open to us" except to "coop-
erate creatively with the forces of convergence toward
global consciousness." Like Teilhard, he expects that
the global consciousness "will not level all differences
among peoples; rather it will generate . . . creative
unions in which diversity is not erased but intensified."

This consciousness is to be global also in another
sense—in rediscovering its roots in the earth. "The
future of consciousness, or even life on the earth, is
shrouded in a cloud of uncertainty by the pollution
of our environment, the depletion of natural resources,
the unjust distribution of wealth, the stockpiling
of nuclear weapons." If we do not attain the new
consciousness "rapidly," Cousins warns, we will "perish from the earth."

We must, therefore, rediscover the pre-Axial Age's
consciousness, which was "collective, and cosmic, rooted

in earth and life cycles," and integrate that into the "self-reflective, analytical, critical consciousness [of] the First Axial Period." Tribal consciousness must now see "humanity as a single tribe, . . . related organically to the total cosmos." Cousins is not suggesting "a romantic attempt to live in the past"; he is saying, rather, that "the evolution of consciousness proceeds by way of recapitulation."[28] The sonata form is at the core of his Hegelian type of evolution of consciousness.

Cousins's expectation has been a pivotal belief in the Baha'i Faith for a century and a half. William S. Hatcher and J. Douglas Martin write in *The Baha'i Faith: The Emerging Global Religion* that the "central message" of Baha'u'llah, the Faith's founder, "is that the day has come for the unification of humanity into one global family." God has set in motion an historical process that will result in "the emergence of a global civilization." Baha'u'llah called for "the creation of an international auxiliary language, which would allow every society to maintain its own cultural identity while benefiting from the ability to communicate with all other races and nations."[29]

Still, I do not think that a Second Axial Age is upon us. First, most people, I among them, have no sense of humanity's impending self-destruction, and thus Cousins's cause for a change in consciousness is absent in us. Second, we would not necessarily make or seek the change even if we feared that our present consciousness was leading us to perish soon. We might, indeed, perish; nothing persuades me that humanity is destined to exist. I do not share Cousins's rationalistic and optimistic faith in human nature.

Third, there are alternatives besides self-destruction or global consciousness. We might keep our individualistic consciousness and seek solutions such as military deterrence, political compromise, economic treaties, scientific and technological progress—or prayer.

Fourth, I see no sign anywhere of a global consciousness, present or forthcoming. It has not appeared even in an area of global interdependence, the economy. For instance, Robert J. Samuelson wrote the following in October 1998:

> It's possible to glimpse recovery in today's weakening world economy—but only barely. For all the anguish over the global crisis, there remains a curious absence of urgency. The Japanese have dithered over banking reform. Europeans generally seem unconcerned, despite the threat to the huge trade surplus that has kept their economy expanding. . . . And American anxieties have been mostly rhetorical. When it has come to action— Congress's approving IMF funds, the Fed's cutting interest rates—the pace has been unworried and unhurried.[30]

From a later perspective, when the world economy was in its longest period of continuously rising prosperity, we can see that the nations of 1998 were right not to be anxious about a possibility of an impending self-destruction of their economy.

Cousins sees a Second Axial Age approaching because he embraces a utopian myth. But I would like to know, for example, what he considers a "just distribution of wealth," and why? Those not lured by the sirenic myth, by the hope of a return to perfect wholeness, see us at an intermediate stage of the only Axial Age thus far.

Finally, the basic problem that Cousins sees as arising only now has actually confronted us since the start of the Axial Age: how to integrate our consciousness of individuality with our social and older nature. We are still far from a resolution. Our social nature has generated diverse attempts at vicarious returns to wholeness in our social relations, and the fear and thrill of our consciousness of individuality have generated diverse views of a vicarious return to wholeness in our relationship to the cosmos. These are two types of life meanings: one ethical, one metaphysical.

A life meaning, then, is an intraested involvement that returns one vicariously to primordial wholeness. It originates with birth, and it becomes a problem with one's emerging sense of individuality. This sense originated, historically, at the beginning of the Axial Age. No actual return to primordial wholeness is possible, and no meaning of life is certain; but probing one's life meanings is important for self-realization, for those who "choose life." "*Self*-realization" means more than a realization of the *individual*; it means a realization of the *person*, whose basic nature is social as well as individual.

Today's populace neither deliberates over life meanings, nor faces the ubiquitousness of uncertainty; it escapes from the risks of individuality into an automatic certitude in society's life meanings, though it does not relinquish the sense of individuality. But when anomy and egoism destroy that certitude, suicide increases.

A Second Axial Age would perhaps prevail should the populace face its incapacity to attain certainty and deliberate over its meanings of life, conscious of their uncertainty. But I see no hint of such a change in consciousness. Hence, all that remains for me to do in this book is to shed more light on my own meanings of life.

Chapter 6

Epilogue

I begin from the feeling and fact of uncertainty. We cannot attain certainty about facts, values, or life in general. Our limited degree of knowing, which is part of our pervasive finitude, is fixed in the substance and attitude of my life meanings. And yet the meanings are not without satisfaction.

I believe that the universe has no purpose. Science has not found any evidence of a cosmic purpose because that is not within its purview[1], nor has philosophy provided a good argument. Still, such purpose is a possibility, though, for me, a negligible one. Once, a long time ago, following my religious tradition, I believed that a Creator had endowed the universe with meaning. But vast unredeemable cruelty destroyed my faith in a cosmic purpose and a just, let alone merciful, Almighty.

Hence, I am metaphysically lonely. Metaphysical loneliness is a feeling that existence is nobody's friend, that we are all vagrants in the universe. It emerges with an awareness that human existence is inherently conflicting, unable to support happiness for long, and that, ultimately, every person is alone. Such loneliness is not a mere accompaniment to personal tragedy or to the absence of friends; it is an obbligato to the consciousness of the human condition, arriving with the understanding that all blessings are hexed— that Utopia is "no place," as its Greek etymology signifies, not because it is imaginary, but because it is unimaginable.

Such a world is absurd: it is deaf to our cries, and it is laughable. It evokes "metaphysical laughter" in some, in me, which Elie Wiesel describes and ascribes to the hasidic master, Rebbe Nahman of Bratzlav (1772–1811):

> Laughter that springs from lucid and desperate awareness, a mirthless laughter, laughter of protest against the absurdities of existence, a laughter of revolt against a universe where man, whatever he may do, is condemned in advance. A laughter of compassion for man who cannot escape the ambiguity of his condition and of his faith. To blindly submit to God, without questioning the meaning of this submission, would be to diminish Him. To want to understand Him would be to reduce His intentions. How then can man take himself seriously? Revolt is not a solution, neither is submission. Remains laughter, metaphysical laughter. . . .[2]

Metaphysical laughter varies, however, and mine differs from Rebbe Nahman's. Mine, also, began as a "protest" and "revolt" over the absurdities of existence, but it is no longer that; for with whom shall I grapple, since I no longer believe in a Creator? Rebbe Nahman, however, was a *zaddik,* so he could protest to God.

Mine, also, is a "laughter of compassion," but it is for senseless hurt, and not for the general "ambiguity of our condition." For ambiguity is often a condition of truth, beauty, and freedom, and I cherish that and those. Ambiguity challenges dogma, simplism, and despotism. It is a species of uncertainty that can approach the ultimate nature of reality—complexness.[3]

Also unlike Rebbe Nahman's metaphysical laughter, mine is not always "mirthless." Sometimes, when I turn from earthly matters and gaze at the night sky, stars illumine the ultimate mysteries: why is there anything rather than nothing at all, and why is anything not different? I am then face to face with cosmic purposelessness, with metaphysical absurdity, because these questions cannot be answered, and a metaphysical laughter of soft irony emerges because I know that these questions can never be answered. This laughter is not mournful.

My metaphysical laughter is sometimes directed to the irony of inherited loyalty. For instance, my loyalties to Judaism and Zionism most likely would not have arisen had my parents been Muslims instead of Jews. I am assuming that, apart from religion, my parents would have retained their characters, personalities, socioeconomic status; and yet these life-meaning loyalties would have been unthinkable, and my life could have been quite different.

How can I not laugh at the irony of deep loyalties turning on accidents of birth and birthplace? How can I not laugh at the folly of vain disputes over contrary inherited loyalties? Neither laughter is sorrowful. But my metaphysical laughter does become "mirthless" when these disputes turn into injustice, war, terrorism, assassination, or other violence.

Still, I cannot rest with metaphysical laughter. Neither its woe nor its clamor nor its haughtiness satisfies me. I can laugh with Erasmus at the folly of others, but such demeanor demeans me if sustained; and if sustained does not sustain me. But if metaphysical laughter does not suffice, then what remains? Remains dignity, metaphysical dignity.

Metaphysical dignity arises when a sense of self-worth nobly faces the absurdity of existence. For example, it prevails when I, as a single one, respond with "the courage to be" on facing an unknowing and uncaring world; or when I laugh at my own folly, since I demonstrate self-worth as the one who laughs; or when abandoning God because of the Holocaust, since I maintain self-respect as the one who resists the temptation of flimsy or obscene theodicies.

I do not wish to suggest that only atheists can acquire metaphysical dignity. I know several traditional rabbis who exhibit metaphysical dignity by rejecting every theodicy in the face of the Holocaust's concrete enormities, though they believe that the universe has some inscrutable God-given meaning. Instead, they endure silently and work against evil. The belief that humans are made "in the image of God" supports their sense of self-worth.

Rebbe Nahman knew the absurdity of existence in the *shtetl* long before the Holocaust. He said: "Hell exists not in the other world, but here. Only no one dares to admit it." Even "when the Messiah will come, nothing will change, except that people will be ashamed of their foolishness." No theodicy would have dared to approach him! His strong sense of self-worth was also evident earlier in chapter 4, in Louis Jacobs's observation that Rebbe Nahman "dared to criticize Maimonides for his philosophical leanings, not an uncourageous thing to do in his age." He also expressed metaphysical dignity in a buffoonery that mocked himself and God's universe. Wiesel describes this as follows:

> . . . He played with the urchins to mock the Rebbe inside him. He played war to show the absurdity of wars. He posed as a madman to deride reason and appearances, and as a penniless nomad to underline the grotesque aspect of possessions. He played the clown to rid himself of the last vestiges of pride that persisted inside him. All this he could not do where he was known. That is why, at home, he went to the other extreme: he disarmed his pride by pushing it to its limits, by exaggerating his own importance in all areas . . . He deliberately made himself into a caricature. . . .[4]

I had to include the three preceding paragraphs even though the subject of this chapter is *my* life meanings. For one easily gathers that metaphysical dignity is for me also an ethical ideal, even though the present focus is metaphysical, and I could not chance an impression that religious persons are incapable of such dignity. Furthermore, the paragraphs indicate metaphysical dignity's wide range of response: from the quiet and conventional to the loud and shocking.

One's own death is a conspicuous aspect of the absurdity of existence. Death is absurd because we know that its finality is inevitable and yet we crave physical immortality. Metaphysical dignity arises here, then, when a sense of self-worth nobly faces the absurdity of one's imminent death. I do not know whether I shall die with such dignity.

Voluntary martyrs die with much metaphysical dignity because they exhibit great trust in their judgment about life's meaning. Terroristic suicide-bombing, however, is heinous, utterly without ethical dignity. Life meanings in the Axial Age are ultimately chosen, in a sense, even when they are inherited, unquestioned, and unconscious because one has chosen not to question them; but martyrs face their life meanings dramatically.

Others manifest self-worth at dying in quieter contexts. They die quite peacefully, feeling that life has been worthwhile despite all the absurdities, that they have adequately satisfied their axiological (which includes the ethical) life meanings. They, too, die with metaphysical dignity. Still others manifest self-worth in unbearable, hopeless, and dehumanizing sickness by ending their life.

Metaphysical dignity is a metaphysical life meaning that requires me to be true to my axiological life meanings; it bridges metaphysical and axiological life meanings. Indeed, its definition links the "absurdity of existence" to the values of "self-worth" and "nobleness." Metaphysical dignity integrates life and death. It is contrapuntal: it is a separate melody in the metaphysical and axiological spheres of life meaning, and a harmony of the two. The music of these spheres is a vicarial return to primordial wholeness.

Rilke's mood is similar:

> *Affirmation of life AND death* appear as one in the 'Elegies.' . . . Death is the side of life that is turned away from us: we must try to achieve the fullest consciousness of our existence, which is at home in the *two unseparated realms, inexhaustibly nourished by both.*[5]

Metaphysical dignity is an "affirmation of life AND death" that encourages us to "try to achieve the fullest consciousness of our existence"—of our axiological and metaphysical life meanings. It integrates life and death; it is "nourished by both."

Dignity is the essence of ethics, morality in a concentrated form: Treat others with the dignity that you desire for yourself. This means: Be honest, just, kind, and respectful with others and yourself, for all of us are born worthy beings.

Dignity is more than the essence of ethics; it is the essence of nearly all humanism. For humanism puts the highest worth on humanity and its capacity for noble conduct, works of art, and systems of thought. Truth, beauty, goodness, and creativity are thus humanistic ideals, and they are for me the supreme expressions of dignity.

Alas, many restrict the term *humanism* to a "nontheistic, rationalist" outlook, and the dictionary gives them a secondary recognition. Accordingly, some religious people oppose humanism. But others view much of religion as humanistic, and I agree with them. Emanuel Rackman, for instance, integrates humanism into his theology:

> Judaism places the highest value on man and his potential. But Jewish humanism is not antithetical to the belief in a personal God. On the other hand, it derives from the fact that God created each of us in His image. The supreme worth of man is vouched for in every phase of Jewish law and thought. . . .[6]

Dignity is expressed variously, but not all perceive its full range. For example, some see it as only

interested,[7] while others see it as only intraested.[8] But I
see both interestedness and intraestedness as capable of
expressing dignity. Each allows us to be free in a unique
way: interestedness, to gain mastery, and intraestedness,
to wander, be spontaneous, and welcome novelty. The
humble may inherit the land (Psalm 37:11), but they
do not possess the dignity of those who subdue it
(Genesis 1:28); yet the subduers of earth do not possess
the dignity of those who simply rove its beauty. I seek
a satisfactory balance among the various sorts of dignity
for myself and for humanity.

So, all of my life meanings can be grouped under
humanism. But there are passions that have dominated my daily life for half a century: truth, creativity,
and love. Dignity accommodates these passions, but
it does not embrace love. Love and dignity are imma-
nent in each other, but love also transcends dignity.
Nevertheless, love is not unconditional; it, too, is
uncertain. As Rilke wrote:

> It's one time
> for each thing
> and *only* one.
> Once and no more.
>
> And the same for us:
> *once.*
> Then never again.
>
> But this once having been
> even though only once
> having been on earth
>
> seems as though
> it can't be undone.

Notes

Chapter 1. Intraestedness and Meanings of Life

1. Henry D. Thoreau, "Life without Principle," in *The Portable Thoreau,* ed. Carl Bode (New York: Viking Press, 1947), p. 633.

2. Claire Huchet Bishop, *All Things Common* (New York: Harper and Brothers, 1950), pp. 4, 5, 22.

3. *Ibid.,* pp. 5, 6.

4. *Ibid.,* pp. 6, 7.

5. *Ibid.,* p. 35.

6. A. Bartlett Giamatti, "Giamatti: Talking Baseball," *Newsweek,* November 6, 1989, p. 87 (italics mine).

7. Bruce Brown, *Stephen Pace: Maine and Reminiscences, 1953–1993* (Rockport, ME: Maine Coast Artists, 1994), p. 11.

8. Jerome Eckstein, *Metaphysical Drift: Love and Judaism* (New York: Peter Lang, 1991), chap. XII.

9. Justus Buchler, *Toward a General Theory of Human Judgment,* 2d rev. ed. (New York: Dover, 1979), pp. 18–19.

10. *Ibid.,* pp. 19–21.

11. For instance, Martin Buber, *I and Thou,* trans. Walter Kaufmann (New York: Charles Scribner's Sons, 1970), pp. 83, 95.

12. Emil L. Fackenheim, "The Human Condition after Auschwitz: A Jewish Testimony a Generation After," in *In the Aftermath of the Holocaust*, ed. Jacob Neusner (New York: Garland, 1993), pp. 135–136. For a similar view see also Berel Lang, *Act and Idea in the Nazi Genocide* (Chicago: University of Chicago Press, 1990), pp. 45–46.

13. Jared Diamond, *Guns, Germs, and Steel: The Fates of Human Societies* (New York: W. W. Norton, 1997), p. 39.

14. Sigmund Freud, *Civilization and Its Discontents*, trans. and ed. James Strachey (New York: W. W. Norton, 1961), pp. 36, 39.

15. *Ibid.*, pp. 44, 29–30.

16. Jeffrey M. Masson and Susan McCarthy, *When Elephants Weep: The Emotional Lives of Animals* (New York: Dell, 1995), chap. 10, pp. 192–211.

17. Freud, p. 44. "If one were to yield to a first impression, one would say that sublimation is a vicissitude which has been forced upon the instincts entirely by civilization. But it would be wiser to reflect upon this a little longer."

18. Henri Bergson, *The Creative Mind*, trans. Mabelle L. Andison (New York: Philosophical Library, 1946), pp. 162–163.

19. *Ibid.*, pp. 162, 160–161.

20. Miguel de Unamuno, *Tragic Sense of Life*, trans. J. E. Crawford Flitch (New York: Dover, 1954), pp. 103–104, 234, 122–123.

21. *Ibid.*, pp. 258, 111, 330.

22. Paul Brownback, *The Danger of Self-Love* (Chicago: Moody Press, 1982), pp. 96, 97.

23. The influence of this version of Hillel on Jesus' version in Matthew 7:12 is clear.

24. Erich Fromm, *You Shall Be as Gods* (New York: Holt, Rinehart and Winston, 1966), pp. 58–59; *Man For Himself* (New York: Rinehart and Company, 1947), pp. 129, 131. See my *Metaphysical Drift*, pp. 39–49, for a fuller discussion of the controversy between Brownback and Fromm.

25. Leon Salzman, *Treatment of the Obsessive Personality* (Northvale, NJ: Jason Aronson, 1991), pp. 81, 83. I am grateful to Peter Golden for bringing this book to my attention.

26. *Ibid.*, pp. 83, 82 (italics mine).

27. *Ibid.*, p. 82.
28. *Ibid.*, p. 80.

Chapter 2. Excursus to Objectivity and Postmodernism

1. Moses Maimonides, *The Guide of the Perplexed*, trans. Shlomo Pines (Chicago: The University of Chicago Press, 1963), III. 43, p. 573. Maimonides adds:

> Accordingly, with regard to the *Midrashim*, people are divided into two classes: A class that imagines that [the Sages] have said these things in order to explain the meaning of the text in question, and a class that holds [the Midrashim] in slight esteem and holds them up to ridicule, since it is clear . . . that this is not the meaning of the [biblical] text in question. . . . But neither of the two groups understands that [the Midrashim] have the character of poetical conceits whose meaning is not obscure for someone endowed with understanding. . . .

My father and uncle definitely knew the work of Abraham ibn Ezra, who had anticipated in the Introduction to his commentary on the Pentateuch, the *Sefer Ha-Yashar,* the preceding view of Maimonides; for I heard my father and uncle refer briefly to it once, although I had not yet investigated it. For example, Ibn Ezra criticizes the allegorists, those using the third false method of interpreting Scripture, and concludes:

> Therefore if there appears something in the Torah which seems to contradict reason or to refute the evidence of our senses then here one should seek for the solution in a figurative interpretation. For reason is the foundation of everything. . . . Man's reason is the angel which mediates between him and his God. It follows that wherever we find something in the Torah that is not contrary to reason we must understand it in accordance with its plain meaning and accept it as saying what it seems to say, believing that this is its true meaning. . . .

2. Friedrich Waismann, "Analysis and Metaphysics," *Aristotelian Society Supplementary* 19 (1945): pt. III.

3. Alfred N. Whitehead, *Process and Reality* (New York: Harper Torchbooks/Academy Library, 1960), p. 63.

4. R. Hackforth, *Plato's Phaedo* (Indianapolis, IN: Library of Liberal Arts, 1955), pp. 3–4. For a full discussion of my contention see my *The Deathday of Socrates: Living, Dying, and Immortality—The Theater of Ideas in Plato's Phaedo* (Frenchtown, NJ: Columbia Publishing, 1981).

5. R. S. Bluck, *Plato's Phaedo* (Indianapolis, IN: Library of Liberal Arts, 1955), preface.

6. John H. Randall, Jr., "Plato on the Good Life and Spartan Ideal," *Journal of the History of Ideas*, XXVIII (July–September, 1967): 307–324.

7. Mordecai M. Kaplan, *The Meaning of God in Modern Jewish Religion* (New York: Reconstructionist Press, 3rd printing, 1962), pp. 6–7, 319, 316.

8. *Jewish Week*, February 17, 1995, p. 41.

9. *Massachusetts Lawyers Weekly*, May 28, 1990, p. 1.

10. B. A. G. Fuller, *A History of Philosophy*, rev. ed. (New York: Henry Holt, 1945), p. 217. Bertrand Russell, *A History of Western Philosophy* (New York: Simon and Schuster, 1945), p. 704. John H. Randall, Jr., *The Making of the Modern Mind*, rev. ed. (Boston: Houghton Mifflin, 1940), p. 411.

11. Louis Dupré, in *Mystical Union in Judaism, Christianity, and Islam*, eds. Moshe Idel and Bernard McGinn (New York: Continuum Publishing, 1996), p. 6.

12. Barry Smart, "Modernity, Postmodernity and the Present," in *Theories of Modernity and Postmodernity*, ed. Brian S. Turner (London: Sage Publications, 1990), p. 17.

13. Randall, p. 308.

14. Jacques Derrida, quoted in David Lehman's *Signs of the Times: Deconstruction and the Fall of Paul de Man* (New York: Poseidon Press, 1992), p. 23.

15. *Ibid.*, chap. 1.

16. Brian S. Turner, "Periodization and Politics in the Postmodern," in *Theories of Modernity and Postmodernity*, ed. Brian S. Turner (London: Sage Publications, 1990) p. 1.

17. *Ibid.*, pp. 5–6.

18. *Ibid.*, pp. 1–2.

19. Lieteke van Vucht Tijssen, "Women between Modernity and Postmodernity," in *Theories of Modernity and Postmodernity*, ed. Brian S. Turner (London: Sage Publications, 1990) p. 161.

20. Smart, pp. 25–26.

21. Judith Plaskow, "Jewish Theology in Feminist Perspective," in *Feminist Perspectives on Jewish Studies*, ed. Lynn Davidman and Shelly Tenenbaum (New Haven, CT: Yale University Press, 1994), p. 66 (italics mine).

22. Hava Tirosh-Rothschild, "Feminism and the Discipline of Jewish Philosophy," in *Feminist Perspectives on Jewish Studies*, ed. Lynn Davidman and Shelly Tenenbaum (New Haven, CT: Yale University Press, 1994) p. 113, n. 24.

23. Eugene B. Borowitz, *Choices in Modern Jewish Thought*, 2d ed. (West Orange: Behrman House, 1995), pp. 287–288.

24. *Ibid.*, p. 303.

25. Richard Rorty, a postmodern pragmatist, eschews *objectivity* in the sense of having an "immediate [knowledge of] a nonhuman reality"; for there is "no way of formulating an *independent* test of accuracy of representation––of reference or correspondence to an 'antecedently determinate' reality..."—and this makes the metaphysical controversy between idealists and realists, between subjectivists and objectivists, insoluble. But if one takes objectivity in the pragmatic sense, as "the desire for as much intersubjective agreement as possible," he says, "then one will drop the question of how to get in touch with 'mind-independent and language-independent reality.'" He agrees with Wittgenstein that "questions which we should have to climb out of our own minds to answer should not be asked" (Richard Rorty, *Objectivity, Relativism, and Truth* [Cambridge, England: Cambridge University Press, 1991], pp. 21, 6, 23, 13, 7).

Rorty agrees also with Thomas S. Kuhn's statements that it doesn't help to imagine "that there is some one full objective, true account of nature and that the proper measure of scientific achievement is the extent to which it brings us closer to that ultimate goal" because "there is no theory-independent way to reconstruct phrases like 'really there.'" Hence, he enlists Kuhn in the "campaign to drop the objective-subjective distinction altogether." But Rorty is disappointed that Kuhn draws back from this position when he "asks for an explanation of 'why science works,'" of "why

natural science is so good at predicting," because such an explanation would have to be theory-independent (*Ibid.*, pp. 38, 40).

However, besides the pragmatic rendition of *objectivity*, the
word also has the advantage of pointing toward the unknowable
reality. Rorty considers that a disadvantage. But I think that we are
uniquely and eminently human when wondering intraestedly about
ultimate mysteries without hope of an explanation––such as, why
there is anything rather than nothing, or why, ultimately, anything
is not otherwise. One may wonder with Kuhn why, ultimately,
science works, but one ought not ask for an explanation. The
Psalmist could have said also about such intraested wonder what he
said about our interested prowess: "What is man, that Thou art
mindful of him? . . . Yet Thou hast made him but little lower than
the angels . . ." (Psalm 8: 5–6).

26. Eugene B. Borowitz, *Renewing the Covenant: A Theology
for the Postmodern Jew* (Philadelphia: Jewish Publication Society,
1991), pp.76, 22 (italics mine).

27. Borowitz, *Choices in Modern Jewish Thought*, pp. 293,
296, 289 (italics mine).

28. David Lehman, *Signs of the Times: Deconstruction and the
Fall of Paul de Man* (New York: Poseidon Press, 1992), p. 77.

29. T. R. Martland, "post-modernism—or what's become of
us, tarzan," in *The Antioch Review* 49, no. 4 (Fall 1991): 596–597.

30. Justus Buchler, *The Main of Light: On the Concept of
Poetry* (New York: Oxford University Press, 1974), pp. 92–93.

31. Justus Buchler, *Nature and Judgment* (New York: Columbia University Press, 1955), pp. 15, 17.

32. Emanuel Rackman, *One Man's Judaism* (New York: Philosophical Library, 1970), p. 10.

33. Garry Wills, *Papal Sin: Structures of Deceit* (New York:
Doubleday, 2000), pp. 44, 239–240, 249, 255.

Chapter 3. Suicide and Meanings of Life

1. For instance, Steve Taylor concludes:

While the approach adopted here is in important . . . respects
different from, and critical of, that employed by Durkheim,

I have tried to show why his work remains so important to
our understanding of suicide. In this context it is perhaps
a little ironical that a work begun many years ago with . . . an
ambition to "disprove" Durkheim's "positivist" study of
suicide should end in agreement with many of his funda-
mental principles, especially, that why some people kill
themselves while others go on living are not separate questions, but two sides of the same problem. (*Durkheim and
the Study of Suicide* [London: Macmillan, 1982], p. 196)

David Lester writes:

Durkheim can be faulted on many grounds. He decided
upon appropriate meanings in particular societal associa-
tions so that his theory would be supported. His statistical
analyses were naive by present-day standards. He failed to
provide any guidelines for operationalizing the theoretical
concepts. . . .

Nonetheless, the influence of Durkheim's work on
sociologists who have considered the problem of suicide is
illustrated by the degree to which subsequent sociological
thought on suicide has been dominated by his theory.
Almost every new contribution has attempted in some way
to clarify, develop, or modify some part of Durkheim's
theory. . . . Durkheim's theory has thus stood the test of
time quite well. (*Suicide from a Sociological Perspective*
[Springfield, IL: Charles C. Thomas, 1989], pp. 22, 40)

Colin Pritchard observes:

Modern research on the interrelationship of "economic di-
sasters" . . . and suicide and suicidal behavior continues to
validate Durkheim's great insight (Brenner, 1983; Platt, 1984;
Dooley et al., 1989; Pritchard 1992a; Fischer et al., 1993),
and Warr and Jackson's (1988) finding of what we describe
as the *defensive apathy* of the long-term unemployed, is an
almost exact concordance of what Durkheim predicted.

Invaluably, Durkheim, even while identifying major
social factors, never lost sight of other interactive factors

that might lead some people to suicide, though perhaps he *under*-stated them. His genius is seen in the fact that despite the passing of a hundred years since the first publication of *Le Suicide*, his main premise, though perhaps not its detail, remains intact. One wonders how many social scientists' contributions will still have relevance and validity in a hundred years from now. (*Suicide—the Ultimate Rejection?—A Psycho-Social Study* [Buckingham, England: Open University Press, 1995], p. 92)

Talcott Parsons considers Durkheim's theory of the integration of social systems, of what holds societies together, to have been "nothing short of epoch-making," and whose "full implications . . . have not yet been entirely assimilated by the relevant professional groups." Critical analysis does not refute his theory; "it involves only extension and refinement" ("Durkheim's Contribution to the Theory of Integration of Social Systems," in *Emile Durkheim, 1858–1917*, ed. Kurt H. Wolff [Columbus: Ohio State University Press, 1960], pp. 118, 151).

Kay Redfield Jamison writes: "Emile Durkheim observed last century that there was greater seasonality in suicides in rural areas than in urban ones, a finding replicated earlier in this century in the United States and within the past few years in South Africa" (*Night Falls Fast: Understanding Suicide* [New York: Alfred A. Knopf, 1999], p. 208). I am grateful to Jeffrey Berman for bringing this book to my attention.

2. Emile Durkheim, *Suicide: A Study in Sociology*, trans. John A. Spaulding and George Simpson (Glencoe, IL: Free Press, 1951), p. 246.

3. *Ibid.*

4. *Ibid.*, pp. 247, 248–249.

5. *Ibid.*, p. 252 (italics mine).

6. *Ibid.*

7. *Ibid.*, pp. 252–253.

8. *Ibid.*, pp. 253–254.

9. *Ibid.*, p. 254.

10. *Ibid.*, pp. 254–255, 257.

11. *Ibid.*, pp. 258–262, 271, 273.

12. *Ibid.*, p. 256.

13. Frank Pearce, *The Radical Durkheim* (London: Unwin Hyman, 1989), p. 135.

14. Durkheim, p. 258.

15. Parsons, p. 144.

16. *Ibid.*, pp. 143–144.

17. Durkheim, p. 258.

18. *Ibid.*, pp. 157, 155, 159.

19. *Ibid.*, pp. 159, 160 (italics mine).

20. Durkheim, *Le Suicide: Étude de Sociologie* (Paris: Presses Universitaires de France, 1930), pp. 160, 170; *Suicide*, p. 168.

21. Durkheim, *Suicide*, pp. 159–160. Durkheim may be paraphrasing another assimilated Jew, Flavius Josephus, whom he quotes in another regard (p. 170, n. 25). Josephus wrote of his contemporary Jews (first century C.E.): "Starting from the very beginning with the food of which we partake from infancy and the private life of the home, he [Moses] left nothing, however insignificant, to the discretion and caprice of the individual" (*The Works of Josephus*, vol.1, *Against Apion*, trans. H. St. J. Thackeray [Cambridge: Harvard University Press, 1961], p. 363).

Durkheim's portrayal leaves *little* free judgment to the individual, and Josephus's leaves *none*. Both portrayals are wildly exaggerated. Perhaps Durkheim was reacting to an upbringing in which the rabbinic ideal of doing everything for the sake of God had been taken literally.

22. *Ibid.*, p. 156.

23. Huston Smith, *The World's Religions*, rev. ed. (San Francisco, CA: Harper San Francisco, 1991), pp. 272 ff., 276 ff., 282 ff., 286 ff., 288 ff., 293 ff., 296 ff., 299.

24. Durkheim, *Suicide*, pp. 158–159.

25. *Ibid.*, p. 162.

26. *Ibid.*, pp. 162–163, 167.

27. *Ibid.*, p. 167. I have been unable to find such comparative statistics for the present day, but I conjecture that the widespread Jewish assimilation to the general culture in our day has increased the relative rate of Jewish suicides. I conjecture also that the right-wing Orthodox have the lowest rate of suicide among today's Jews.

28. *Ibid.*, pp. 167–168.

29. A Mishnah concludes that one who studies Torah gains as much reward in this world and the next as does one who fulfills

the combined precepts of peace, benevolence, and honor to parents (Peah 1:1). But Torah study is not considered meritorious for one who does not intend to follow its precepts. The Talmud explains R. Jose's apothegm as: "Whoever says that he has only [an interest in the study of] Torah [but not in keeping its precepts], . . . he has no [reward] even [for the study of] Torah" (Yev. 109b).

For an incisive discussion of Torah study's cognitive and devotional dimensions, see Norman Lamm's scholarly book, *Torah Lishmah—Torah for Torah's Sake: In the Works of Rabbi Hayyim of Volozhin and His Contemporaries* (New York: Yeshiva University Press, 1989).

30. The Talmud relates the following: "R. Tarfon and the Elders were once reclining in the upper story of Nithza's house in Lydda when this question was put to them: 'Which is greater, study [of Torah] or practice [of the precepts]?' R. Tarfon replied: 'Practice is greater.' R. Akiva replied: 'Study is greater, for it leads to practice.' Then they all answered: 'Study is greater, for it leads to practice'" (Kid. 40b).

This was not merely an academic or theological question. The Soncino edition adds the following footnote: "This was a practical problem during the Hadrianic persecution, when both study and practical observance were forbidden, and the question was for which risks should sooner be taken." This was an instance of Durkheim's "general law."

31. Maimonides (twelfth century C.E.) held that Torah study (or keeping any precept) because of fear of punishment is fit only for a child or an ignoramus. Adults should strive to study for the sake of God, to study simply because such is God's wish, and that is no easy matter. But to study Torah as a way of being in God's presence is most high, rare, and difficult.

For a discussion of these Maimonidean views, see chapters 7 and 8 in my *Metaphysical Drift: Love and Judaism* (New York: Peter Lang, 1991).

32. Abraham J. Heschel speaks of this with pride and sympathy even for the "freethinking Jews" of Eastern Europe:

The masses of East European Jews repudiated emancipation when it was offered at the price of disloyalty to Israel's traditions. Both pious and freethinking Jews fought for a dignified existence, striving to assure the rights of the community, not only those of the individual. They manifested a collective will for a collective aim. With lightning rapidity, they straightened their backs and learned to master the arts and sciences. Gifts for abstract dialectic thinking, developed in the course of generations, were carried into scientific research. Hasidic enthusiasm was sublimated in the noble profundity of musical virtuosos. Three thousand years of history have not made them weary. Their spirits were animated by a vitality that often drove them into opposition to accepted tenets. (*The Earth Is the Lord's* [New York: Harper Torchbooks, 1966], pp. 104–105)

33. Heschel relates the following (*Ibid.*, p. 46.):

"Once I noticed," writes a Christian scholar, who visited the city of Warsaw during the First World War, "a great many coaches on a parking-place but with no drivers in sight. In my own country I would have known where to look for them. A young Jewish boy showed me the way: in a courtyard, on the second floor, was the *shtibl* of the Jewish drivers. It consisted of two rooms: one filled with Talmud-volumes, the other a room for prayer. All the drivers were engaged in fervent study and religious discussion. . . . It was then that I found out . . . that all professions, the bakers, the butchers, the shoemakers, etc., have their own *shtibl* in the Jewish district; and every free moment which can be taken off from their work is given to the study of Torah. And when they get together in intimate groups, one urges the other: '*Sog mir a shtickl Torah*—Tell me a little Torah.'"

34. Parsons, p. 147.
35. Durkheim, *Suicide*, pp. 217, 221.
36. *Ego* in Greek and Latin signifies simply "the person speaking or writing," whereas *altruisme* is derived in French from *autrui*, "of or to others," and from the Latin *alter*, "another."

I have written elsewhere about this invasion of morality into language with regard to words whose original meanings signified only position in space ("The Fall and Rise of Man," in the *Journal for the Scientific Study of Religion* V, no. 1 [Fall 1965]: 68–81).

37. Durkheim, *Suicide*, pp. 221, 219, 227, 217–219.

38. *Ibid.*, pp. 223, 222; *Le Suicide*, p. 240.

39. *Ibid.*, pp. 223–225.

40. Karl Jaspers, "The Axial Age of Human History," *Commentary*, 6 (November 1948): 430.

41. Quoted by Marc-Alain Ouaknin in *The Burnt Book: Reading the Talmud*, trans. Llewellyn Brown (Princeton, NJ: Princeton University Press, 1995), p. xiv. I am grateful to Howard A. Cohen for bringing this book to my attention.

42. *Ibid.*

43. Huston Smith, *The World's Religions*, rev. ed. (San Francisco, CA: Harper San Francisco, 1991), p. 113.

44. Durkheim, pp. 221, 227; *Le Suicide*, pp. 245–246.

45. *Ibid.*, p. 227.

46. Jerome Eckstein, *The Deathday of Socrates: Living, Dying, and Immortality—The Theater of Ideas in Plato's Phaedo* (Frenchtown, NJ: Columbia Publishing, 1981).

47. Durkheim, p. 276.

48. Kay Redfield Jamison, *Night Falls Fast: Understanding Suicide* (New York: Alfred A. Knopf, 1999), pp. 21–22, 45.

49. *Newsweek*, July 1, 1996, p. 59.

50. Durkheim, *Suicide*, p. 227.

51. Perry Meisel faults R. D. Laing for "always hesitat[ing] to ask: whether or not self and other even exist except in their relation." Meisel also believes that Daniel Burston (in *The Life and Work of R. D. Laing*), like Laing, "is unable, or unwilling, to integrate this paradox into his thinking" (*New York Times Book Review*, September 8, 1996, p. 13). I do not think that it is even a paradox.

52. Jaspers, p. 431. William Weifenbach calls this new element "emancipatory consciousness," in his *The Crucible of Consciousness*, an unpublished manuscript.

53. Jaspers, p. 434.

54. *Ibid.*, pp. 432, 431, 432–433.

55. Smith, p. 271.

56. Robert M. Seltzer, *Jewish People, Jewish Thought* (New York: Macmillan, 1980), pp. 34, 50.

Louis Dupré also notes this: It is the "dialogal model that determines the entire [Jewish] religion," for "all relation to God is conceived in the form of an exchange" (in *Mystical Union in Judaism, Christianity, and Islam*, eds. Moshe Idel and Bernard McGinn [New York: Continuum Publishing, 1996], pp. 6–7, 23).

57. David Rosenberg and Harold Bloom, *The Book of J* (New York: Grove Weidenfeld, 1990), pp. 46, 33 (italics mine).

58. Moses Maimonides, *The Guide of the Perplexed*, trans. Shlomo Pines (Chicago: University of Chicago Press, 1963), p. 152; I.62.

59. Emanuel Rackman, "The Right to Privacy in Jewish Law," *Justice* 8 (March 1996): 45.

60. Jaspers, p. 432.

61. Durkheim, *Suicide*, pp. 237–238.

62. Joseph B. Soloveitchik, *Halakhic Man* (Philadelphia: Jewish Publication Society of America, 1983), p. 102. I am grateful to Howard Joseph for reminding me of this quotation.

63. Norman Lamm, "The Face of God: Thoughts on the Holocaust" (New York: Yeshiva University, Department of Holocaust Studies, 1986), sec. 6.

Chapter 4. Uncertainty, Religion, and Meanings of Life

1. Eliezer Berkovits, *Faith after the Holocaust* (New York: KTAV, 1973), pp. 70–71.

2. Adin Steinsaltz, *The Essential Talmud*, trans. Chaya Galai (New York: Basic Books, 1976), p. 11.

3. Emanuel Rackman, *One Man's Judaism* (New York: Philosophical Library, 1970), p. 186.

4. *Ibid.*, pp. 186–188.

5. Steinsaltz, pp. 10–11.

6. Joan DeJean shows that the "Moderns" had already abandoned the premodern view of history in the "culture wars" of the seventeenth century's last decades. *Ancients against Moderns: Culture Wars and the Making of a Fin de Siècle* (Chicago: University of Chicago Press, 1997).

7. René Descartes, *Meditations*, trans. John Veitch (La Salle, IL: Open Court, 1955), Meditation III, p. 49.

8. David Hume, *A Treatise of Human Nature*, ed. L. A. Selby-Bigge (Oxford, England: Clarendon Press, 1960), Bk. I, pt. III, sec. XV, p. 173.

9. Mark Hulliung, *The Autocritique of Enlightenment: Rousseau and the Philosophes* (Cambridge, MA: Harvard University Press, 1994), pp. 7, 8. DeJean also notes this: "In France, the period during which the Culture Wars were waged was the first age to be confronted with the obligation of understanding itself as an era, an entity stylistically distinct from those that had preceded it" (*Ancients against Moderns*, p. 20).

10. Hulliung, pp. 21, 92, 127.

11. *Ibid.*, cited in pp. 52, 57.

12. *Jewish Week*, August 10, 1990), p. 22.

13. Cecil Roth, *A Bird's-Eye View of Jewish History*, rev. ed. (New York: Union of American Hebrew Congregations, 1954), pp. 173–174.

14. Steinsaltz, p. 130.

15. Louis Jacobs notes that the talmudic accounts of Rav are "not always factual and include much that is reported second- or third-hand and therefore to be treated with caution" (*The Jewish Religion: A Companion* [New York: Oxford University Press, 1995], p. 411). This does not, however, weaken my argument, for my argument aims to persuade those who take such accounts literally and unhistorically.

Still, we also find a statement attributed to Rav in which he takes the opposite, unhistorical, view (Yoma 28b): "Rav said: 'Our patriarch, Abraham, kept the whole Torah [long before it was given at Sinai], as it is written, *Because Abraham hearkened to My voice and kept My charge, My commandments, My statutes, and My laws* [Gen. 26:5].' " This supports Jacobs's observation, but it also supports my disputants' view.

Perhaps, though, this attribution was made by a conservative troubled over the liberal attributions. In any case, some ancient talmudic sage, even if not Rav, transcended his Age's concept of history.

16. Fredrick Engels, *Socialism: Utopian and Scientific*, trans. Edward Aveling (New York: International Publishers, 1935), pp. 31, 34, 32.

17. Thus, Steinsaltz writes (p. 24): "The name *tanna* means one who studies, repeating and handing down what he has learned from his teachers. . . . The scholars of the age were overmodest in adopting this title, since in fact this was an epoch of vital independent creativity in many spheres and of innovation of form and content."

18. Louis Jacobs, *Hasidic Thought* (New York: Behrman House, 1976), pp. 231, 230, 58.

19. Louis Jacobs notes that "the major sources for Hillel and his activity are the Talmud and the Midrash and a good deal of the material in these sources dates from no earlier than the time of their compilation, often centuries after Hillel." Hence, "great caution is . . . necessary when using these sources for a reconstruction of Hillel's life and work" (*The Jewish Religion: A Companion*, p. 241).

20. *Jewish Week* (January 2, 1998), p. 11; *Ibid.*, September 10, 1999), p. 40.

21. Moses Maimonides, *The Guide of the Perplexed*, trans. Shlomo Pines (Chicago: University of Chicago Press, 1963), III. 32, p. 526.

22. *Ibid.*

23. *Ibid.*, pp. 529–530. For a further discussion of this issue, see my *Metaphysical Drift: Love and Judaism* (New York: Peter Lang, 1991), chap. 7.

24. Rackman, p. 48.

25. Maimonides, III. 32, pp. 527, 528–529.

26. *Ibid.*, p. 527.

27. *Ibid.*, p. 529.

28. Cited in Elie Wiesel's *Souls on Fire*, trans. Marion Wiesel (New York: Random House, 1972), p. 74.

29. In *Maimonides: The Guide of the Perplexed: An Abridged Edition*, trans. Chaim Rabin (New York: East and West Library, 1978), p. 29.

30. Jacobs, *The Jewish Religion: A Companion*, pp. 307–308.

31. Maimonides, *The Guide of the Perplexed*, trans. Shlomo Pines, III. 27, p. 510; III. 26, pp. 509, 508.

32. Jacobs writes that it is difficult to "reconstruct the life of Rabbi Eliezer" because "he is, like all the other early Rabbinic figures, a hero of Jewish legend, from which it is far from easy to disentangle the facts. Hence, it is surprising that practically all the historians accept at face-value the Talmudic story" under discussion. "The truth is that these stories are very late and were told

possibly centuries after Rabbi Eliezer" (*The Jewish Religion: A Companion*, p. 143).

I agree with Jacobs, but this does not affect my argument because I wish to show my imaginary interlocutors that there is room for humanistic creativity in halakhah even according to their literal and unhistoric reading of sacred text. Moreover, I wish to show such creativity as being a very old tradition, and that would be true even if this story had originated centuries after Rabbi Eliezer.

33. Rackman, p. 177.

34. The editor of the Soncino translation notes in our story the following disagreement between two modern scholars:

> The character of R. Eliezer is hotly contested by Weiss and Halevi. The former, mainly on the basis of this story, . . . severely castigates him as a man of extreme stubbornness and conceit, who would brook no disagreement from his youth until death, and ever seeking quarrels. . . . Halevi . . . energetically defends him, pointing out that this is the only instance recorded in the whole Talmud of R. Eliezer's maintaining his view against the majority. He further contends that the meekness with which he accepted his sentence, though he was sufficiently great to have disputed and fought it, is a powerful testimony to his humility and peace-loving nature.

This disagreement supports Jacobs's observation on the difficulty of "reconstruct[ing] the life of Rabbi Eliezer" (n. 32). Hence, I think that we can speak only of the Talmud's Rabbi Eliezer, and not of the historical life and character of Rabbi Eliezer. I have argued similarly in two books that we should be wary of finding the historical Socrates in Plato's Dialogues; we can speak only of the Platonic Socrates.

35. Maimonides, III. 32, p. 530.

36. Nathan Glazer, *American Judaism*, 2d ed. (Chicago: University of Chicago Press, 1972), p. 135.

37. *Ibid.*, p. 148 (italics mine).

38. Alan T. Davies in *Auschwitz: Beginning of a New Era? Reflections on the Holocaust*, ed. Eva Fleischner (New York: KTAV, 1974), p. 62.

39. Rackman, p. 17.

40. Norma Baumel Joseph, *Separate Spheres: Women in the Responsa of Rabbi Moses Feinstein* (Ph.D. diss., Concordia University, Montreal, 1995), pp. 503, 551.

41. Karen Armstrong, *The Battle for God* (New York: Ballantine Books, 2000), pp. 369, 368.

42. *Ibid.*, p. 371.

Chapter 5. Wholeness: Primordial and Vicarial

1. Rainer Maria Rilke, *Duino Elegies*, trans. David Young (New York: W. W. Norton, 1978), Eighth Elegy, pp. 73–76, 72. I am grateful to Donna M. Main for suggesting these verses as relevant to my thesis.

2. *Ibid.*, Ninth Elegy, pp. 77–78, 80–82.

3. *Ibid.*, Notes and Comments, p. 99.

4. *Ibid.*, Ninth Elegy, pp. 82–83.

5. *Ibid.*, Introduction, p. 13

6. *Ibid.*, Ninth Elegy, pp. 83–84.

7. *Ibid.*, Tenth Elegy, pp. 85–86.

8. *Ibid.*, Introduction, p. 10.

9. *Ibid.*, Tenth Elegy, p. 86.

10. *The Dialogues of Plato*, trans. B. Jowett, 4th ed. (Oxford, England: Clarendon Press, 1953), I, pp. 521–524; *Symposium*, 189d–193 (italics mine).

11. T. S. Eliot, *Four Quartets* (New York: Harcourt, Brace & World, 1943), p. 59.

12. Cited in Nahum N. Glatzer's *The Judaic Tradition* (Boston: Beacon Press, 1969), p. 443.

13. Friedrich Nietzsche, *Beyond Good and Evil*, 65a, in *Basic Writings of Nietzsche*, trans. and ed., Walter Kaufmann (New York: Modern Library, 1992), p. 269.

14. Felix Salzer, *Structural Hearing: Total Coherence in Music* (New York: Dover, 1962), I, p. 211. I am grateful to Ida Faiella-Finclair for bringing this book to my attention.

15. Charles Rosen, *Sonata Forms* (New York: W. W. Norton, 1980), pp. 17, 12.

16. *Ibid.*, pp. 16–17.

17. Rosen notes that the sonata form is a "closed, ordered structure" that "remains a conservative force" even in Chopin's sonatas. Moreover, he observes, "the prestige of the [sonata] form was a conservative force in the history of Romantic and post-Romantic music" that "acted as a brake on the most revolutionary developments" (*Ibid.*, pp. 320, 317, 293).

18. William James, *Pragmatism*, in *Pragmatism and Other Essays* (New York: Penguin Books, 2000), p. 31.

19. *The Dialogues of Plato*, trans. B. Jowett, 4th ed., I, pp. 278, 284–285; *Meno* 81a–82a, 85d–86b.

20. Plato, *Statesman*, trans. J. B. Skemp (Indianapolis, IN: Liberal Arts Press, 1957), pp. 28–29, 31; 271c–272d, 274a.

21. Jerome Eckstein, *The Platonic Method: An Interpretation of the Dramatic-Philosophic Aspects of the Meno* (New York: Greenwood, 1968), pp. 75–79.

22. *The Dialogues of Plato*, trans. B. Jowett, 4th ed., II, p. 497; *Republic*, 619b–d (italics mine).

23. Jerome Eckstein, *Metaphysical Drift: Love and Judaism* (New York: Peter Lang, 1991), p. 51.

24. Paul E. Tsongas, *Journey of Purpose* (New Haven, CT: Yale University Press, 1995), p. 1.

25. *New York Times Book Review*, November 21, 1999, p. 22.

26. Articles on science's current support of religion's belief in a purposeful universe have appeared in several news magazines. For instance, *U. S. News & World Report* (July 20, 1998) concludes its cover story as follows: ". . . the trend line of cosmology unquestionably favors a sense of purpose. Existence may be eternal, prewired somehow for life; consciousness may expand forever . . . ; there may be a larger cosmic enterprise waiting for us to join its purpose, if we can just learn wisdom and justice" (p. 52). What anemic support—all those "may be"s and a trend that is questionable!

Now, for specifics. "Physicist Ernest Sternglass . . . recently argued that the propitious circumstances of the big bang show that the universe is 'apparently designed for the development of life and destined to live forever . . .'" (p. 52). For example, the article reports: "Researchers have calculated that after a big bang, unless the ratio of matter and energy to the volume of the universe . . . was within one-quadrillionth of 1 per cent of the ideal, runaway relativity would have rendered the cosmos uninhabitable . . ." (p. 48).

Sternglass "concludes" that the big bang is designed for the development of life, however, only because his hidden premise is that life, particularly human life, had to come into existence. That premise makes the delicate balance of the big bang's circumstances appear to be a supernatural design, but the premise begs the question. We who refuse to beg say simply that had the big bang been different then life would not have come into existence. The universe shows no sign of being designed for a purpose.

The article also reports that "Allan Sandage, one of the world's leading astronomers, [says] that contemplating the majesty of the big bang helped make him a believer in God, willing to accept that creation could only be explained as a 'miracle'" (p. 52). But such majesty is neither necessarily a supernatural phenomenon, nor proof of God's existence or of cosmic purpose. Sandage's "conclusion" is also smuggled in a hidden premise.

The articles do not report that some of the believing scientists mean by "God" an impersonal Theory of Everything, a mathematical formula that would explain all, and not a supernatural Personal Being. These scientists consider science and theology as parallel disciplines that do not intersect. Indeed, the universe is silent on the existence of a personal God or a cosmic purpose. The cosmos is not anthropic; some scientists are anthropocentric, and they would profit from reading David Hume's eighteenth-century philosophic *Dialogue Concerning Natural Religion*.

27. Karen Armstrong, *The Battle for God* (New York: Ballantine Books, 2000), pp. 167–169.

28. Ewert H. Cousins, *Christ of the 21ˢᵗ Century* (Rockport, ME: Element, 1992), pp. 7–8, 9–10.

29. William S. Hatcher and J. Douglas Martin, *The Baha'i Faith: The Emerging Global Religion*, rev. ed. (Wilmette, IL: Baha'i Publishing Trust, 1998), pp. xv, 44. I am grateful to Betsey Belvin and Harris Snoparsky for bringing this book to my attention.

30. Robert J. Samuelson, "The Crash of 1999?", *Newsweek*, October 12, 1998, p. 31.

Chapter 6. Epilogue

1. See chap. 5, n. 26.

2. Elie Wiesel, *Souls on Fire*, trans. Marion Wiesel (New York: Random House, 1972), pp. 198–199.

3. Justus Buchler focuses on the ultimacy of complexness throughout his *Metaphysics of Natural Complexes* (New York: Columbia University Press, 1966).

4. Wiesel, pp. 198–199.

5. Rainer Maria Rilke, *Duino Elegies*, trans. David Young (New York: W. W. Norton, 1978), p. 10.

6. Emanuel Rackman, *One Man's Judaism* (New York: Philosophical Library, 1973), p. 149.

7. For instance, Joseph B. Soloveitchik, agreeing with the Psalmist, writes: ". . . dignity was equated by the Psalmist with man's capability of dominating his environment and exercising control over it" (*The Lonely Man of Faith* [New York: Doubleday, 1992], p. 15).

8. For instance, Abraham J. Heschel writes:

In the tempestuous ocean of time and toil there are islands of stillness where man may enter a harbor and reclaim his dignity. The island is the seventh day, the Sabbath, a day of detachment from things, instruments and practical affairs as well as attachment to the spirit. (*The Sabbath*, 7th printing [New York: Farrar, Straus and Giroux, 1981], p. 29).

Index

Abecassis, Armand, 60
absoluteness, 40–41, 66,
  72, 79, 96, 104
  See also certainty; perfection; pureness;
  utopianism
act, 10–12, 21, 62
afterlife, 20, 134
ambiguity, 77, 79, 133
Armstrong, Karen, 105,
  124
art, 2, 13–14, 15, 43, 81
Axial Age, 3
  and the consciousness of
  individuality, 58–59,
  66–69, 71, 108, 113,
  118, 124–125
  and critiques of society,
  81
  and life's meanings, 66–
  67, 118, 136

and myths, 119–121
and religion, 124
and suicide, 61
and wholeness, 122

Baal Shem Tov, 116
Baha'u'llah, 126
balance
  in Bergson, 16
  between objectivity and
  subjectivity, 32, 40, 44
  in dignity, 138
  in Durkheim, 57, 64
  in Freud, 15
  in interests and intraests,
  2, 24–25, 11–12
  and life meanings, 44,
  61
  and love, 15, 70
  and situations, 64–65
Barbu, Marcel, 8